D1548333

THE PRENDERGAST LETTERS

The Prendergast Letters

CORRESPONDENCE FROM

FAMINE-ERA IRELAND,

1840–1850

Edited by
SHELLEY BARBER

University of Massachusetts Press · *Amherst & Boston*

Copyright © 2006 by the Trustees of Boston College
All rights reserved
Printed in the United States of America

LC 2006008286
ISBN 1-55849-550-9
Designed by Jack Harrison
Set in Adobe Caslon with Ovidius display by Dix
Printed and bound by The Maple-Vail Book Manufacturing Group

Library of Congress Cataloging-in-Publication Data

Prendergast, James, d. 1848.
[Correspondence. Selections]
The Prendergast letters : correspondence from famine-era Ireland, 1840–1850 /
edited by Shelley Barber.
    p. cm.
A collection of forty-eight letters in the manuscript collection of the
John J. Burns Library, Boston College, chiefly written by James Prendergast
to his children, with the correspondence being continued after his death
by his widow Elizabeth Prendergast.
Includes bibliographical references and index.
ISBN 1-55849-550-9 (cloth : alk. paper)
1. Prendergast, James, d. 1848—Correspondence.
2. Prendergast, Elizabeth, d. 1857—Correspondence.
3. Prendergast, James, d. 1848—Family. 4. Kerry (Ireland)—History—19th century—Sources.
5. Kerry (Ireland)—Social life and customs—19th century—Sources.
6. Famines—Ireland—History—19th century—Sources.
I. Prendergast, Elizabeth, d. 1857. II. Barber, Shelley, 1960–
III. Boston College. John J. Burns Library. IV. Title.
DA955.P74 2006
941.9'60810922—dc22
                          2006008286

British Library Cataloguing in Publication data are available.

This book is published with the support and cooperation of the John J. Burns Library,
Boston College, Chestnut Hill, Massachusetts.

CONTENTS

ILLUSTRATIONS

PREFACE

The Special Irish Collection in the John J. Burns Library of Rare Books and Special Collections at Boston College was formally established in 1948 with the bequest of a large collection of Irish books and manuscripts from the estate of Boston attorney John Hughes, a prominent figure in the Boston Irish community. It has grown to become the largest, most comprehensive Irish research collection in America. One of the Library's most prized Irish treasures is a collection of forty-eight letters from Ireland between 1840 and 1850, primarily written or dictated by James and Elizabeth Prendergast of Milltown, County Kerry, Ireland, to their children in Boston. It would appear that descendants of James and Elizabeth Prendergast were responsible for the donation of these letters, but there is no clear documentation to this effect.

Although the Prendergast letters represent a rare and important firsthand, contemporary account of the effects of the Great Hunger, *An Gorta Mór*, they remained largely a well-kept secret until Professor Kevin Whelan, Burns Library Visiting Scholar in Irish Studies, 1995–96, published a selection of them in connection with an article he wrote for the *Boston College Magazine*, titled "Bitter Harvest: What the Famine Stole from Ireland" (Winter 1996). Interest in the Prendergast letters mushroomed following the publication of Whelan's article. Burns staff member Shelley Barber took a special interest in these letters and set out to transcribe the entire collection, originally to make them more accessible to users in the Library. Her passion and enthusiasm for this undertaking proved contagious, however, and it was soon decided that her transcriptions should be published. The historian Ruth-Ann Harris, a member of the Irish Studies faculty at Boston College, and the genealogist Marie E. Daly, Director of Library User Services at the New England Historic Genealogical Society, graciously volunteered to contribute their expertise to the publication. The former agreed to write a prefatory essay focusing on the

Prendergast family in Ireland, and the latter contributed a brief history of the Prendergast family in America. The result of this collaborative effort is a major scholarly contribution not only to Famine studies but also to Irish American studies.

It is has been my pleasure to witness and encourage the extraordinary collaborative efforts of editor Shelley Barber and historians Ruth-Ann Harris and Marie Daly in bringing this publication to completion. Theirs has been a labor of love, and I am very grateful for their unselfish commitment not only to make the contents of these letters more readily available but also to put them in historical perspective. The Burns Library is proud to see in print another one of its special collections, and I congratulate those who made this possible, most especially Shelley Barber, Ruth-Ann Harris, and Marie Daly.

I wish to acknowledge with gratitude the generous financial support received from the Ian Anstruther Publication Fund of the Burns Library and from Paul and Denise Delaney of Duxbury, Massachusetts.

ROBERT K. O'NEILL
Burns Librarian

ACKNOWLEDGMENTS

The expertise and encouragement of many individuals made this book possible. Every member of the staff at the Burns Library contributed toward this publication. In particular among them I thank David Horn, who invited me to take on the project and offered support throughout the work; Robert O'Neill, who made this publication possible; and John Atteberry, who not only shared his expertise but allowed so much of my time to be spent away from the Reading Room. In addition, I am very grateful to the following people for their interest in the collection and for their time and valuable assistance: Thomas O'Sullivan, Mary Leinenbach, Mary Maher-Shaw, William Spring, Valerie Bary, and Prendergast descendants Megan Newman and Patricia Mulhern and their families. I am grateful for the work of Edward McCarron and the assistance of Marie Daly, Peter Gray, Ruth-Ann Harris, Margaret Kelleher, Brian Ó Conchubhair (and his folks in Tralee!), Kevin Whelan, and student staff at the Burns Library, particularly Lisabeth Buchelt. I am especially grateful to Paula Corpuz and Doug Clanin of the Indiana Historical Society, whose review of the method of transcription was invaluable, and to Paul Wright and Carol Betsch of the University of Massachusetts Press, for their skillful guidance. Finally, I wish to thank my family: my parents, Robert and Margaret Barber, for always encouraging my interest in family history and the history of Boston, and my daughter, Jennie Stowe Dineen (a Boston Irish girl with roots in County Kerry), for graciously sharing her mother with the family of James and Elizabeth Prendergast.

SHELLEY BARBER

THE PRENDERGAST LETTERS

Introduction to the James Prendergast Family Correspondence

SHELLEY BARBER

*T*HE PRENDERGAST LETTERS in the manuscript collection of the John J. Burns Library, Boston College, consist of forty-eight documents, most of them written in Ireland between 1840 and 1850 and sent to members of the family in Boston, Massachusetts. This publication includes transcriptions of all the letters in the collection.

James and Elizabeth Prendergast of Milltown, County Kerry, Ireland, were the parents of John, Maurice, Michael, Julia, Jeffrey, and Thomas. Prior to her emigration, Julia Prendergast married Cornelius Riordan. During the period of the correspondence Julia and Cornelius lived in Boston, where they were joined by her brothers Jeffrey and Thomas. The majority of the letters were sent to these children by their father. His widow continued the correspondence after his death in 1848 until her emigration in 1850. Other writers of the letters were Maurice, Thomas, Michael, and Michael's wife Ellen.

The letters demonstrate the importance of such communication during this period of mass emigration. Over a hundred individuals, other than immediate family members, are named in the correspondence. The letters ask for and offer information about neighbors on both sides of the Atlantic. They convey details of weather, crops, local economy, and banking and postal services. The politics of the day, including the proposed Repeal of the Act of Union and the trial of Daniel O'Connell, are mentioned. There are accounts of illness, births, and deaths. Family members in Ireland acknowledged the receipt from Boston of over £139 in monetary assistance. It is clear that this money was the means of preserving the family. The letters are most notable for the descriptions they contain of the potato blight, subsequent years of famine and hardship, and the response of the family, community, and nation to these extraordinary circumstances.

The earliest letter in the collection, a character reference written for Thomas Prendergast by his employer in Ireland prior to his emigration, was not mailed and must have been carried by Thomas to Boston. The letters mailed to Boston were addressed to Thomas or Jeffrey Prendergast or Cornelius Riordan, though they were primarily intended for all of the children in Boston, rather than for individuals. They were mailed from post offices in Milltown, Tralee, and Killarney. There is one reference to a hand-carried letter, but this, if it reached its destination, is not extant. The final letter in the collection was sent from Liverpool, England, by Elizabeth prior to her embarkation as she made her journey to America. The only letter, other than Thomas's letter of reference, which was not mailed to Boston was sent by his brothers to Michael in St. John, New Brunswick, in 1847.

Though a few of the letters are torn and portions therefore are missing, they are otherwise in excellent condition. Each is written on a single sheet of paper. Most are four pages long, written on two leaves. The first page of each letter bears the address. They were folded for mailing and sealed with wax. There is often slight damage to the paper where the letters were sealed. There were no stamps affixed, but postage paid was noted on the address leaf of each letter, together with postal cancellations that were stamped along the route from Kerry to Boston. These stamps vary in legibility. They include the post offices where the letters were mailed, Liverpool, and New York. The majority of the letters bear four to seven such stamps. These have not been included in the transcription.

Most of the letters in the collection were dictated by Prendergast family members to scriveners. With few exceptions, the handwriting and spelling are not difficult to decipher, though the fact that they were dictated often results in awkward sentence structure. Two local men are named within the letters as scriveners. One was Daniel Connell, a schoolteacher, and the other was his relative by marriage, Patrick D. Mahoney, who identifies himself as a land surveyor. There may have been other professional scriveners. Letters that differ in language and handwriting style from those written by Connell and Mahoney include those sent by Maurice, and by Michael's wife Ellen.

One postscript written and signed by James Prendergast shows that he was literate, though his choice to pay scriveners indicates that he may not have had sufficient skill to write the fairly lengthy letters that he regularly sent. Michael and Ellen's children attended school in Milltown, and it is possible that their daughter Julia may also have acted as scrivener. Most of Elizabeth's letters appear to have been written by Connell. A small selection of letters has been reproduced in this volume to illustrate the differing styles of language and handwriting that occur throughout the correspondence.

It is not known how Boston College came to own the collection. In 1909, Jeffrey's son James Maurice Prendergast donated money to Boston College toward the construction of the first buildings on the Chestnut Hill campus.[1] In the 1930s, after James Maurice's death, his sister, Julia Catherine Prendergast, is recorded as having donated money in her own name and in memory of her brother to the Boston College Library toward the purchase of the Seymour Adelman Francis Thompson Collection.[2] This collection remains a cornerstone of the Burns Library's holdings. James Maurice and Julia Catherine Prendergast were members of the New England Historic Genealogical Society. The siblings' philanthropic work and monetary donations to various institutions were numerous. This generosity, combined with their interest in their family heritage and their familiarity with Boston College's library, suggests that they may have been the donors of the letters.

Portions of fifteen of the letters in the collection were previously published in an article in *Boston College Magazine* 55, no. 1 (Winter 1996). The theme of that issue was the Famine in Ireland and its consequences.

The method of transcription was chosen so as to mimic closely the original documents. The line divisions appear as they were originally written. The letters have been numbered in chronological order, and each of the letters is preceded by this number, along with a brief line of text telling the reader whom the letter is from and which family members are named in the salutation. Following this is the address to which it was sent, if any, and any text that was written on the address leaf. All of the text has been left justified. The original capitalization, spelling, punctuation, superscripts, and underlined words have been retained with the following exceptions:

- Throughout the correspondence are words whose initial letter appears to be capitalized as a result of handwriting style. There are also numerous words in which it is impossible to tell if an initial letter is intentionally capitalized or not. When there is doubt, the letter has been made to conform to modern standard practice.

- There are frequent occasions where sentences clearly end without terminal punctuation. In these cases periods have been added, and the first letters of the following sentences have been capitalized. The choice of where to end these sentences may not always be accurate. There is no indication within

1. Boston College Archives, RG2.13, President's Office Records, Fr. Gasson, Box 1, folder 20.
2. Terrence L. Connolly, S.J., ed., *An Account of Books and Manuscripts of Francis Thompson* (Chestnut Hill, Mass.: Boston College, 1937), [xii].

the transcription to signal the reader that these changes have been made. In any other case where punctuation has been added for clarity, it is bracketed.

- Text that appears in the margin of a page, or has been written over other text, has been inserted where it would be intended to be read and has been described in a footnote.

- In transcribing the addresses, no attempt has been made to recreate the original spacing of words. All of the text, including addresses, signatures, and datelines has been left-justified.

- For the word "and" the writers often use "+." The word "and" has been substituted.

- When a dash is used as a period, a period has been substituted. When a dash is used to fill space at the end of a line, it has been eliminated.

- The symbol resembling a closing brace, }, which is sometimes used following opening salutations, has been replaced with a comma. In the same letters, the salutations are often underlined. These underlinings have been eliminated.

- Interlineations have been retained and are signaled with carets at both ends.

- Canceled words have been retained, with strikethrough.

- Letters, words, or punctuation omitted by the writer in error and added to the transcription for clarity are inserted in brackets.

- Missing words are noted by an ellipsis in brackets. A footnote containing an explanation follows. Where damage to the paper causes several words or lines in a row to be missing, only the first ellipsis in the sequence has an explanatory footnote.

- In words which are abbreviated with superscripted letters (e.g. M^r, Am^t, Rec^d), the periods which sometimes follow the superscripted letters have been eliminated.

- A number of pages of the letters end with the words "turn over." These words, though irrelevant in the transcriptions, are included because they are characteristic of scrivener Patrick Mahoney (letters #6–13, 19, 21).

Textual Devices

ˌadded wordˏ = writer's interlineations

~~word~~ = writer's deletion

[word or letter] = text supplied by editor

[. . .] = missing word(s) (with footnote if needed)

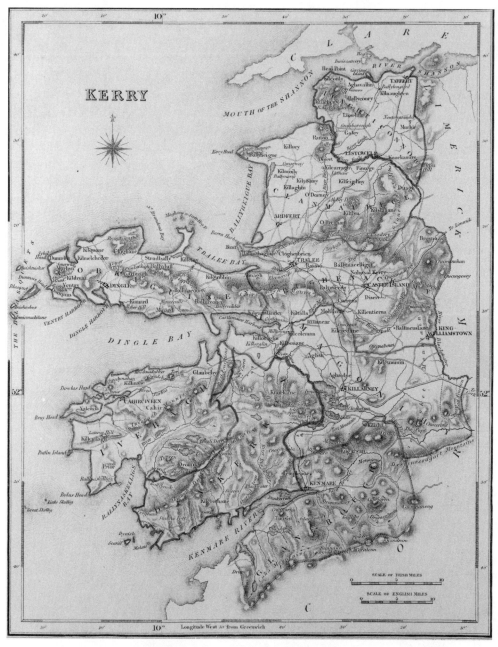

Map of the County of Kerry. (Samuel Lewis, *Lewis's Atlas Comprising the Counties Of Ireland: And a General Map of the Kingdom* [London: S. Lewis, 1848])

The Prendergast Family in Ireland

RUTH-ANN M. HARRIS

> *. . . we are most anxious to hear from you often, as the*
> *receipt of your letter is at the lower calculation a twelve*
> *month younger to us in place of getting old.*
>
> JAMES PRENDERGAST, November 1844

*T*HE PRENDERGAST LETTERS are a rare and almost unique opportunity to study the raw material for judging both the lives of a family in Ireland during the Famine years and the lives of the emigrant children in America. Studies of the immigrant Irish have tended to emphasize either those who became distinguished major figures in America or the relatively undifferentiated mass of those who barely survived. In these letters we learn about various family members who weighed opportunities shrewdly and utilized contacts skillfully to eventually succeed in their adopted country. There is a remarkable degree of family affection as well as family enterprise in the forty-eight letters preserved by the Boston family.

Milltown, home of the Prendergasts, in the parish of Kilcolman, County Kerry, has ancient roots as a meeting place of three roads and the Maine and Laune rivers. In medieval times it was the location of an Augustinian monastery, generally believed to have been established by St. Colman of Cloyne, the patron saint of the town. A thriving commercial center in the mid-eighteenth century, modern Milltown, an observer noted in 1758, had been built by the principal landlord, "Mr. Godfrey," "for tradesmen of all sorts," and he was "endeavouring to establish some trade here for butter and fish for Cork."[1] Many trades flourished, but Milltown was early renowned for its linen industry, reputedly established in medieval times by a family of McCrohans from Valentia.[2] Sometime after 1793, John Godfrey, whose wife Eleanor Cromie came from a County Antrim linen family, tried to restore linen-making, which had

---

1. Patrick O'Sullivan, *I Heard the Wild Birds Sing: A Kerry Childhood* (Dublin: Anvil Books, 1991), 192.

2. Valerie M. Bary, "A Short History of Milltown," in *Milltown Parish, A Centenary Celebration*, ed. Thomas Egan (Naas, Ire.: Leinster Leader, 1994), 38–50; Valerie M. Bary, "The Square at Milltown," *Kerry Magazine*, no. 12 (2001): 15–18.

failed. The town again became a center of linen production, which left its mark in still-existing place-names such as Bleach Road.[3] But by the 1820s the linen industry in Ireland was once more faltering, unable to compete against cheaper manufactured goods flooding the market from the more efficient English cotton mills. Linen was not the only economic activity, however. Cooperage was an important occupation, as Milltown was a supplier to the Cork butter market, and there was also a forge that served the wider community.[4]

The Prendergasts resided on Bleach Road, which suggests that the family may have come from elsewhere, attracted by opportunity.[5] There is a strong family connection to nearby Killarney. Records show that some of the family members married and had their children baptized there (and the letters show that the friends and family of daughter Julia Prendergast's husband, Cornelius Riordan, worked and resided in Killarney).

Temporary migration was the lifeline of many Irish families in this era. Particularly in the west of Ireland, seasonal migration to the grain-growing areas of the eastern counties and to England was a mainstay of the pre-Famine economy.[6] Large numbers of males from Kilcolman, in contrast to adjoining parishes, migrated seasonally to other counties.[7] Linen manufacture was likely to have been at low ebb during the growing season, thereby requiring laborers

---

3. Bleach Road developed a negative reputation in the 1920s and 1930s; one parish priest commented on the behavior of courting couples there: "Wherever the devil is by day, he's in Bleach Road by night" (O'Sullivan, *Kerry Childhood*, 198).

4. O'Sullivan, *Kerry Childhood*, 197.

5. Royal Commission on Condition of Poorer Classes in Ireland: first report and appendices, Appendix A, Supplement; Appendix B, Medical Relief, Dispensaries, Fever Hospitals, Lunatic Asylums; Supplement, Parts I and II, Sessional papers, 1835 (369), p. 227. The evidence of Sir John Godfrey to the Poor Law Commissions was that the parish was unusually needy. In his words, about twenty-five widows lived by chance employment and fifteen others lived by charity. There were a hundred beggars in the area. About twenty-five to thirty males migrated seasonally—most didn't go to England.

6. For a study of the role of seasonal migration in the transnational economy of Ireland and England, see Ruth-Ann M. Harris, *The Nearest Place That Wasn't Ireland, Early Nineteenth-Century Irish Labor Migration* (Iowa: Iowa State University Press, 1994).

7. Evidence for this may be found in the 1835 Inquiry which was undertaken by asking standardized questions of "knowledgeable informants"—clergymen, magistrates and the like—in a sample of parishes within each barony of the country. Among the questions included in this valuable survey were those relating to whether seasonal migration was an important practice, how many persons were engaged in such migration, and whether persons from that parish migrated to England. Geographer and folklorist Anne O'Dowd has used this evidence in her book, *Spalpeens and Tattie Hokers, History and Folklore of the Irish Migratory Agricultural Worker in Ireland and Britain* (Dublin: Irish Academic Press, 1991).

to seek agricultural work elsewhere during periods of peak demand for farm labor. Accounts of the employment status of Prendergast family members in the letters suggest that they used personal contacts to find work. They did relocate to find jobs and housing, but remained within County Kerry. An important local family, the Eagars,[8] employed at least four of the Prendergast sons. John worked for Charles Agar in Tralee, Thomas worked for Dr. John Agar in Killarney before he emigrated, Maurice worked for attorney Richard Eagar and for the Eagar family in the Killarney area at Curraglass and Glenflesk, and Michael also worked for a time at Curraglass.

In whatever way James Prendergast had made his living as a young man, by the time he and Elizabeth lived on Bleach Road he had to supplement their meager resources by leasing agricultural land. James wrote in February 1841 (in the first extant letter, 18 months after Thomas and Jeffrey arrived in Boston) that he had leased a new piece of garden land to add to one already under cultivation. We don't know his age, but he was quite an elderly man who reported frequent serious illnesses. What resources besides his uncertain strength could James draw on to cultivate this land? In addition to the occasional and expected help from his three remaining sons and their children, James may have employed laborers with the money remitted home from the Boston family. But when times were tight and the Boston money insufficient, James was forced to borrow from "a worthy friend."[9]

Survival was precarious in these pre-Famine years, and the Irish often turned to emigration when migration was no longer possible. In Milltown, emigrants to North America were leaving in considerable numbers well before there was an established pattern of emigration from the rest of County Kerry. Taking data from the Boston *Pilot* "Missing Friends," we find searches for sixty individuals from the parishes of Kilbonane and Kilcolman,[10] many of whom were reported to have left Milltown prior to 1845. This is at least twice the incidence in the surrounding parishes.

It is hardly surprising that the children of the enterprising Prendergast family were among those from Kerry seeking greater opportunity abroad. After their only daughter, Julia, and her husband Cornelius Reardon emigrated to Boston, the two youngest were the first sons to leave. Unlike their

---

8. Members of the family spelled the surname both Eagar and Agar.

9. Letter #4, 27 July 1841.

10. Milltown was near the border of Kilbonane and individuals sought were reported to be from Kilcolman or Kilbonane.

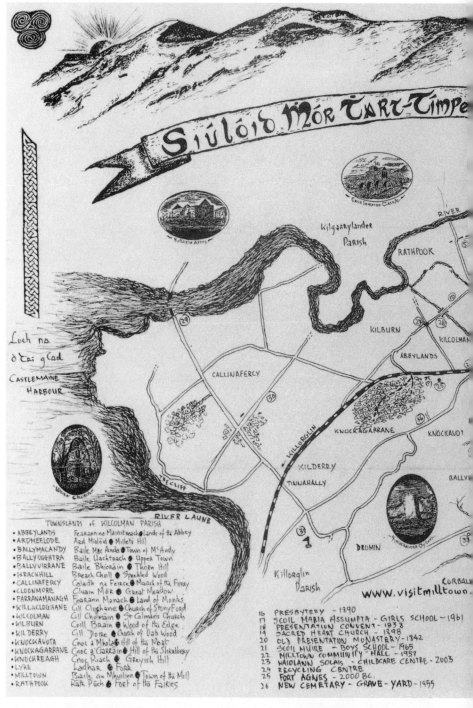

Siúlóid Mór Tart-Tímpeall Baile an Muílinn (Great walk around Milltown)
by Thomas O'Sullivan (Map courtesy of Thomas O'Sullivan)

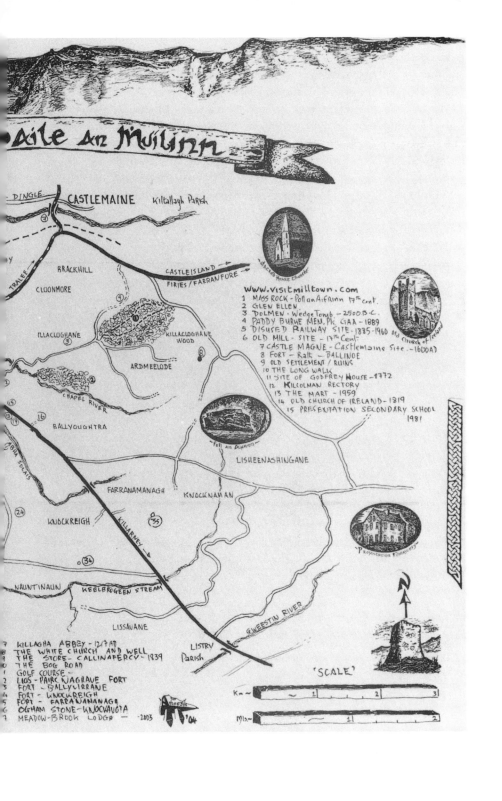

áile an Muilinn

DINGLE — CASTLEMAINE — Kiltallagh Parish

BRACKHILL

CLOONMORE

TRALEE

ILLACLOGHANE

KILLACLOGHANE WOOD

ARDMEELODE

CHAPEL RIVER

BALLYOUGHTRA

ABIA SOLAIS

FARRANAMANAGH — KNOCKNAMAN

KNOCKREIGH — KILLARNEY

NAUNTINAUN — KEELBROGEEN STREAM

LISSAUANE

GWEESTIN RIVER

LISTRY Parish

CASTLEISLAND →
FIRIES / FARRANFORE →

LISHEENASHINGANE

www.visitmilltown.com
1. MASS ROCK - Poll an Aifrinn 17th cent.
2. GLEN ELLEN
3. DOLMEN · Wedge Tomb - 2500 B.C.
4. PADDY BURKE MEM. Pk. GAA - 1889
5. DISUSED RAILWAY SITE - 1835-1960
6. OLD MILL - SITE - 17th Cent.
   7. CASTLE MAGNE - Castlemaine Site - 1600 AD
   8. FORT - Rath - BALLINOE
   9. OLD SETTLEMENT / RUINS
   10. THE LONG WALK
   11. SITE OF GODFREY HOUSE - 1772
      12. KILCOLMAN RECTORY
      13. THE MART - 1959
      14. OLD CHURCH OF IRELAND - 1819
         15. PRESENTATION SECONDARY SCHOOL
                                             1981

"Sacred Heart Church"

Old Church of Ireland

"Poll an Dúnan"

"Presentation Primary"

7. KILLAGHA ABBEY - 1217 AD
8. THE WHITE CHURCH AND WELL
9. THE STORE - CALLINAFERCY - 1939
10. THE BOG ROAD
11. GOLF COURSE -
12. LIOS - PAIRC NAGRAVE FORT
13. FORT - BALLYVIRRANE
14. FORT - KNOCKREIGH
15. FORT - FARRANAMANAGH
16. OGHAM STONE - KNOCKVAUOTA
17. MEADOW-BROOK LODGE -   2003

Aneestin '04

N

'SCALE'

Km ~   ~   1   2   3
Mls ~   1   2

older brothers John, Maurice, and Michael, Thomas and Jeffrey were single and thus most free to seek their fortune in America. Thomas carried a valuable "character" with him from his former employer, Dr. Agar.

While the aim of many was to return home with enhanced status, by the 1840s most emigrants would have known that lack of opportunity made return to Ireland less and less feasible. Hoping against hope, however, James expected his sons to return, an expectation reiterated in many of the early letters. In his first letter he reminded Thomas and Jeffrey, "I never will leave this life until I see you here."[11] Responding to requests from his sons for their ages (which they would need to know if they were to take citizenship)[12] James wrote, "Should ye be inclined to remain in that country it would be our wish to be stretched along side ye wherever ye should be, but were ye to come home to the native Isle or if it be your wish why we should like to be intered with the Forefathers"[13]—probably his way of reminding them that he expected them to return. In October 1842, James wrote of Francis and Edward Spring, local men who had just visited from Boston, "from the enquiry made by your Mother of the Springs of your ever coming home they had told her ye never would."[14] In the following year their parents continue to express their wish to see their children return: "we have some nice hams of old sound Bacon waiting your arrival home together with a good Fat pig which will be fit for sticking after your arrival here. Let us know in your next letter when do ye intend coming home."[15]

Their history and culture gave the Irish a capacity to prosper in a foreign country, for they had long since learned to live under rulers of an alien religion and retained a tenacious popular memory of who they were. In addition, the Prendergast family had experience in actively searching for commercial opportunities. (More than once James advised his sons to draw on connections and abjure companions who would be a bad influence.) And perhaps most important, Thomas and Jeffrey had the support of parents who made it clear that they could return at any time to the family, and were thus not like the immigrants whose families had forced them out into the world.

---

11. Letter #2, 25 February 1841.
12. U.S. District Court Boston Naturalization Petition, 1:123. After two years, immigrants to the United States were expected to make a Declaration of Intent and could take citizenship after five years. Thomas made his declaration of intent in 1844 and his petition for naturalization in 1846.
13. Letter #9, 9 November 1844.
14. Letter #8, 11 October 1842.
15. Letter #10, 12 June 1843.

When Maurice heard that the Boston family was inviting his young son James Maurice to emigrate, both father and grandfather expressed their hopes that James Maurice would prove himself worthy of their support. James Maurice was described to his uncles as "active, strong, and . . . both graceful and grateful"[16] and, later, "clever and well behaved."[17] Decisions to send out children were made carefully. In 1845 Jeremiah Connor, publican of Milltown, asked James to enquire of the prospects for the eldest of his seven children, seventeen-year-old Patt, "a proper honest Boy and a very Proficient scholar." He had heard that apprentices in America were paid, unlike in Ireland. Connor was "most anxious to have the eldest Boy in some good way to get thro life than have him in this miserable country in Poverty."[18]

It is evident that James was able to write because he signed most of his letters and wrote a brief postscript to his letter of 27 July 1841. Nevertheless, he and Elizabeth used scriveners. Presumably many of the letters sent by immigrants or their families in Ireland were written by scriveners, whose presence was usually invisible. One of the chief scriveners hired by the Prendergasts, however, land surveyor Patrick Mahoney, inserted himself in a number of postscripts he wrote, which may explain why he was willing to undertake the task of writing for the family—he frequently requested that Thomas and Jeffrey convey personal messages to his own relatives in Boston.

Newspapers were important in the lives of immigrants, and family members on both sides of the Atlantic mailed local papers to one another. The Prendergast letters include references to the *Pilot*, the *Boston Nation*, the *New England Reporter*, and the *Kerry Evening Post*. The *Pilot*, with its "Missing Friends" section, was one of the earliest and most important newspapers serving the Irish community in America. When their cousin Maurice Prendergast failed to arrive in Boston after leaving Tralee in the renowned vessel the *Jeanie Johnston*,[19] the brothers instituted a search via an advertisement placed in the *Pilot* on 24 March 1855.[20] On another occasion, 8 July 1843, Thomas placed an ad for Cornelius Mahoney, brother of the Prendergasts' scrivener Patrick. In a post-

---

16. Letter #33, 26 September 1847.
17. Letter #39, 29 October 1848.
18. Letter #22, 21 May 1845.
19. The Jeanie Johnston Company, Blennerville, Tralee, County Kerry, Ireland, "The Jeanie Johnston," http://www.jeaniejohnston.ie/home.asp?id=1. The *Jeanie Johnston* (1847–1858) was the most famous of Irish emigrant vessels, famed for never having lost a passenger to disease.
20. Harris and O'Keeffe, *Search*, 3:279.

script to James's letter of August 1843, Patrick wrote, "I am extremely thankful to you and ever will, in the extraordinary trouble you have taken with respect to my Beloved Brother."[21] That the family continued to enjoy the paper is attested to in Thomas Prendergast's obituary in the *Pilot* of 9 February 1895, which noted: "Mr. Prendergast was for many years an earnest reader and admirer of the *Pilot*."[22]

Money is an understandably important topic in the letters. Quite simply, James reiterates again and again that the old parents' survival depended on the money sent home. Each sum received was scrupulously recorded and acknowledged. References to letters that do not survive tell us that the amounts mentioned in the extant letters are not the total sum of what was sent, but amounts reported from 1841 through 1850 equal £139 or US $2,318.18 (converted to today's buying power, $15,746.50).[23] James and Elizabeth expected their children to send money home, as was Old Country custom. James reinforced this belief when he wrote critically of emigrant neighbor Margaret Forhan, now in Boston, "Neither she [nor her] Brothers sent a single penny tho' their Mother really wants [needs] it."[24] James also wrote to his children to advise their cousins John and Larry Ford that their mother in Cork was "very poorly situated. . . . Speak to them and let them know the entire matter. It would do them credit if they sent her a trifle."[25]

Gratitude fills the letters from the senior Prendergasts, who in return sought to give what they could to their children. Mother Elizabeth knitted stockings for her Boston children. In his letter of May 1841, James writes that she had tried to send stockings with Mrs. Fleming, "who prepared to go out last March" but was thwarted when a friend, John Gnaw, reneged on his promise to fund her trip (so the stockings "remain[ed] in Cork Hill").[26] In September 1841, James wrote that Mrs. Fleming now planned to leave on the first of April and would take nine pair of stockings. In his April 1842 letter, he reported that Elizabeth had sent another fifteen pair by John Quirk, and the children could be assured that "they were all knitted by your affectionate

21. Letter #11, 3 August 1843.
22. Obituary of Thomas Prendergast, *Pilot*, 9 February 1895.
23. Robert Sahr, Inflation Calculator, *Columbia Journalism Review*, http://www.cjr.org/tools/inflation/. Calculations were devised by first converting pounds to dollars, then adjusted for inflation.
24. Letter #25, October 1845.
25. Letter #17, 18 July 1844.
26. Letter #3, 29 May 1841. It appears that Mrs. Fleming may have been a widow. John Gnaw may have been willing to fund her emigration in exchange for taking over her lease of land.

Mother."[27] By August, James was expressing concern that none of them had acknowledged receipt of the stockings. More were sent with emigrating neighbors until the Boston family must have protested, since James wrote in July 1844 that "Your Mother feels hurt at desiring her to send no more stockings. She says she would feel a pleasure in knitting them for ye."[28]

James and Elizabeth's letters convey their values through their judgments and advice about people. James noted the impecunious funeral of a man whose wife's dowry was still in the bank: "Roger Sheehy . . . as I was Informed Died in poverty though having money in Bank by the wife. . . . The coffin which was around him was more like a county coffin falling asunder at conveying him to his natural Burying place."[29] In several letters James warned his sons against neighbors they might encounter in Boston: "I dread ye may lose anything with John Gnaw. Beware yourself of him. He behaved a great skeamer."[30] Of the young coachman to Sir William Godfrey who was accused of stealing money from his employer and consequently shipped out to Boston, James warned, "beware of him—keep yourselves civil and strange to him."[31] On another occasion he instructs his children to "Beware of John Flynn. . . . He is what we commonly call a trickey."[32]

Many of the letters were addressed to Julia's husband, possibly because he was literate and other members of the family were not. In his first letter, James says that her mother wants to know if Julia keeps a servant, which may have been a way of asking if the couple were prospering. As an only daughter among five sons, Julia's emigration would have left her aging parents bereft, and she was apparently much loved. Her physical condition concerned her mother, and there were many inquiries as to Julia's state of health ("a Killarney woman who came home lately acquainted us that my Dear child Judy was not getting her health in that country," James wrote in September 1841. "Now I hope and trust at the arrival of this letter you will send us an answer mentioning the state of your healths").[33] These frequent questions about Julia's health in particular may have been coded language for expressing concern that the couple continued to be childless.

---

27. Letter #6, 28 April 1842.
28. Letter #17, 18 July 1844.
29. Letter #16, 24 May 1844.
30. Letter #4, 27 July 1841.
31. Letter #16, 24 May 1844.
32. Letter #18, 9 November 1844.
33. Letter #5, 29 September 1841.

The story of son Michael Prendergast and his wife Ellen illustrates what could befall a young family with scarce means in a time of decreasing resources. Marriage in Ireland could only be considered if males and females each brought resources to the union sufficient to establish a viable unit. Males generally brought land, while females brought dowry. The distribution of land and dowry was the prerogative of the senior males of the family, which kept unmarried children subject to patriarchal control.[34] In this pre-Famine world of shrinking resources, marriage was becoming an increasingly precarious venture. Michael's marriage to Ellen Roach may have gotten off to a poor start because relations with his father-in-law were not good, quite possibly the result of a dispute over Ellen's dowry, which may not have been fully paid.[35] (This is suggested by Michael's explanation, "My Fatherinlaw and I does not chime well. What he promised me I did not get which was one of the disappointments.")[36] His financial problems worsened when his sheep were stolen. With the help of Patrick Mahoney, the scrivener, unbeknownst to his father, he appealed to his brothers for help. (That Michael, who lived next door to his parents, went behind his father's back to ask his brothers for help suggests the degree of James's patriarchal control over the family.) Michael called upon brotherly ties: "Dear Brothers I intend troubling you a little. As being my first request and I trust as faithful subjects and Brothers you will not fail sending same (ie) the sum of £3..0s.0^d. By remitting me this to purchase a mule would be the greatest means of making me comfortable through life."[37] Appealing to their emotions, he referred to the scene of their parting: "I thought at our last fairwell inside the ditch of the old Pike near Killarney that I would not be so long from seeing you."[38]

Though initially piqued at his son's insubordination, James became sympathetic to his plight and wrote in May 1844 in support of Michael's appeal. The brothers apparently came through, and Michael bought a mule. Later, however, it died after "some Blackguards illtreateing the poor animal."[39] (This suggests that Michael had been earning income from leasing out the mule as a

34. For a study of the role of dowry, see Ruth-Ann Harris, "Negotiating Patriarchy: Irish Women and the Landlord," in *Reclaiming Gender: Transgressive Identities in Modern Ireland,* ed. Marilyn Cohen and Nancy J. Curtin (New York: St. Martin's Press, 1999), 207–25.
35. Families often paid only part of a daughter's dowry so as to ensure her good treatment in her husband's family. Difficulties arose when the wife's family could not complete the payment, which may have been the case for Ellen Roach and Michael.
36. Letter #13, 3 November 1843.
37. Ibid.
38. Ibid.
39. Letter #21, 7 March 1845.

draft animal.) After the loss of the mule, his father-in-law again rebuffed Michael, this time after James approached him, offering to match twelve shillings to purchase another animal. At that time Michael began "preparing to go to that yankey country" but was prevailed upon by his parents early in 1845 to remain in Milltown until the spring of 1847. Taking advantage of the cheapest possible fares by traveling to Canada rather than to the United States, he finally left Milltown to sail from Cork for St. John, New Brunswick, on Easter Monday, 27 March 1847, leaving his wife and four children with very little to sustain them. By December, Ellen wrote to her husband that their family was suffering because the famine relief committee had denied her application: "Me self nor the children got none of the relief [meal] these four months past. The comitee for givun relief came to a plan and kept [meal] from the fameleys of Every man that went to America."[40] Two months later, Ellen gratefully acknowledged thirteen pounds from her husband, which she distributed as he requested among the family. Ellen Prendergast and the children eventually joined Michael in Boston.

Marriage in Ireland was vastly different from marriage in America, as is apparent in Thomas's marriage to Catherine Cotter in Boston. Instead of taking primary responsibility for his son's choice of partner and bargaining on terms for the couple's future, James first heard the news of Thomas's marriage as gossip. In his letter of 20 November 1846, James wrote, "John Payne arrived here some time since. He said ye were well, and that he heard Tom was married, but could not say it absolutely. . . . Ease our troubled minds. Say if either of the boys married."[41] Thomas and Jeffrey understood the implicit reproof, so that when Jeffrey married the next year, James and Elizabeth were forewarned. According to the historian Kerby Miller, the reason for the difference in marriage customs was economic: "greater employment opportunities [in America] . . . enabled farmers' sons and daughters to marry partners of their own choosing rather than according to what the Ulster-American James Richey condemned as 'the old Irish rule to marry for riches and work for love'."[42]

James Prendergast was acutely interested in politics, and in the letters discussed issues from the impending Corn Bill to Daniel O'Connell's campaign to overturn the Act of Union. O'Connell figured largely in Milltown tradition because he had visited the town during his campaigns for full civil rights for

---

40. Letter #34, December 1847.
41. Letter #28, 20 November 1846.
42. Kerby A. Miller, *Emigrants and Exiles: Ireland and the Irish Exodus to North America* (Oxford: Oxford University Press, 1985), 219.

the Irish, and James invariably referred to him as the Liberator.[43] "Repeal is carrying on in great splendour in this country by our Liberator Dan[1] OConnell M.P.," James wrote in August 1843. "We are all in this country Repealers."[44] His letters over the next year are filled with discussions of O'Connell and the contentious issue of Repeal.

The Famine and its depredations are vivid in the letters. The first news of the potato blight was reported in late September 1845, and James wrote in October of that year, "The beginning of this Harverst was very promis[ing]. . . . But within the last few weeks the greatest alarm prevails throughout the kingdom. . . . The potatoes which were good and healthy a few days since are now rotten in the ground. Even some which were dug in beautiful dry weather and stored in Pits seem to be affected with the same blight. . . ."[45] Parliament was called, he wrote, to devise ways to deal with the calamity. By November 1846, there was nothing but "distress and destitution. Famine and starvation threatening everywhere unless God mercifully sends some foreign aid."[46] It is likely that famine conditions contributed to the death of James and Elizabeth's son John in the spring of 1847. John's only surviving child, Elizabeth, then five years old, was orphaned by 1850.

The Prendergasts had ambivalent relationships with their local clergy. Father Batt O'Connor had come to the parish in 1842, following the removal of the very popular priest Father John Quill. When he traveled to Boston in 1847 on a mission to collect funds in the emigrant community for the building of the cathedral in Killarney, James warned his sons, "ye need not lose much to him on our account. We were under no compliment to him."[47] Despite James's cautions, Father Batt was an important link with the children in Boston, returning to Milltown in 1850 with news of the family and items sent to their mother. Elizabeth sought the advice of local priests including Father Batt as she considered leaving Milltown for Boston after James's death.

In America, the younger Prendergasts learned to be the architects of their own fortune. The letters provide insight into the life they left behind, the parents and traditions that gave them a solid foundation and skills which allowed them to succeed in the face of adversity.

---

43. O'Sullivan, *Kerry Childhood,* 124.
44. Letter #11, 3 August 1843.
45. Letter #25, October 1845.
46. Letter #28, 20 November 1846.
47. Letter #33, 26 September 1847.

The Letters

I never will leave this life
until I see you here.

JAMES PRENDERGAST,
February 1941

LETTER I. A character reference for Thomas Prendergast written by his former employer, Dr. John Agar of Killarney. This is the earliest letter in the collection and the only one not by a family member.

1. A character reference for Thomas Prendergast written by his employer, John Agar

Bearer Thomas Prenderghast
lived with me for one year and
a half during which time He
conducted himself soberly, honestly
and with such propriety as is
seldom found in higher classes.
I do not expect to meet with
so good a servant for some
time again. I regret his
leaving me.
Jn Agar MD[1]
April 20/40
Killarney

2. From James Prendergast to his children in Boston

Mr Cornelius Reardon N° 10
No 10 Oliver Street, Boston
N. America

Milltown 25th February 1841

My dear Children
Your Letter of the 30th of December last arrived here
before the first of this month and I am sure I need not say
what pleasure it gave each of your family on hearing from

---

1. Below the signature is a wax seal with a floral emblem.

it that ye were in good health. When your Letter arrived
I was lying very ill, in consequence of some ulcer or very
dangerous lump which I got on the Ribs. After some time
it came to a supuration and discharged a considerable
quantity of fetid matter. My recovery was much dreaded
but at present I am well thank God. This will account
for my delay in answering your letter, as I could not
attempt it sooner. Your Mother and friends are all well.
I have taken a good new Garden in addition to the
redigging which I had. If can seed and till what I
have I may say I would be happy against next
Season. Mrs Fleming will be going this season early.
She carry ye a good supply of socks. She desires to give
ye her best respects. John Ginna[2] (Mrs Ginna's Brother
=inlaw) with his Wife and family are prepared to go over
with some other neighbours. Kitty Keting of Tralee begs
of you enquire for her Brother, Uncle and Sister. They are
somewhere about ye. Father OFlaherty knows them
well. If you can send us word how they are situated
and if they are worth anything. Mich^l desires to let
Jeffrey know that he spent 7 weeks ploughing at Curoglas
and never met with greater kindness. Let me know if
Mary Leahy is doing well and if Jude[3] has any servant
maid. I think if I lived as long as my uncle John
Flahiv who died in December last aged 102 years, I never
will leave this life until I see you here. Tell me if
Con and Jude enjoy good health and how each of you
is at present. Your Brother John has a Daughter called
Jude. Every one of the Boys is in the state ye left them

---

2. This surname occurs throughout the correspondence and is variously spelled *Ginna, Ginnaw, Gnaw,* and *McKenna.*

3. Jude is the daughter of James and Elizabeth Prendergast—Julia Riordan. Persons named Julia are often referred to in the letters as *Judy* or *Jude.*

and they join me in sending ye our love and blessing
I am, dear children, your
affectionate father
James Prendergast
P.S. I desired Roger Sheehy Write to his
Daughter M[rs] Ginna. He and family are all well
but they have no account of his son Mich[l].

3. From James Prendergast to his son Thomas

M[r] Cornelius Riordan
N° 10 Oliver Street
Boston
America

Milltown May the 29th 1841

Dear Thomas, I take the opportunity of writing these
few lines to you hoping to find you and the rest
of the brothers and sister in as perfect state of health as
this leaves me at present thank God. I also rec[d]
your letter of the 15th March last with your remittance
of £5..0[s].0[d] and Dear child it was never so much
wanting as at the moment I received same. Dear Thomas
let Cor[s] Reardan know that I was with his Brother Dan
in Killarney some time ago and he is well in health
and is still in the same place. He told me he Intended
writing to his Brother but he has neglected and he told
me to mention him in my letter. Now I have to acquaint
you that he is void of clothes at present. Dear Thomas
I have double the quantity of Garden sat this year that

I had last year. I had sent some stocking with Mrs
Fleming who prepared last march herself to go and being
seduced by John Gnaw who went last March but when they
arrived in Cork he would not give her the money which
he promised her. The stocking was in her Trunk and
it remains in Cork Hill which she promises daily
to bring them but I have not rec^d them as yet. Your
Brother Maurice is out of his place as Mr Richd Eagar's farm
was ejected. Now he has been highly encouraged by the
Eagars of Glenflesk to go to themselves. Now you have
mentioned in your letter about the post as being so neglectful
in writing. Now I have to acquaint you respecting the postage.
For every letter I pay 1^s at the receipt and the same at the
Entry of one. Also the packet starts from Liverpool on the
first Wednesday of the month to that place ₍ie₎ the states₎ wherein it sails
from Liverpool for different other parts of America three
times a month. That is the cause of our neglect in writing
often to you as nothing would give me and your Dear mother
greater comfort as hearing from you all. I wrote to you two
letters one in the month of march last and another in the month
of April. Let me know in your next letter whether you rec^d
either as it gave me a good deal of uneasiness this time past.
Let me know how Con and Judy are in health and
are they still in the same situation and also you and your
Dear Brother are you in the same situation still. I had
mentioned in one of my last letters about a man named
William Keating Brother to Kitty Keating Darby Sullivan's wife.
I hope you will enquire or whether you know him or would
you be able to make inquiries respecting or what is he.
Your Brother Mich^l has got a young daughter and also
your affectionate Brother John another daughter and
two months before the birth of the female he came from
Tralee to know whether your Dear mother would have

any objection of calling her after his sister Judy. Accordingly
she was called Judy. I remain yours affectionate
Father &c. [. . .]⁴
James Prendergha[. . .]⁵
Milltown
P.S. Now I with your affectionate mother join in
prayers and with our thousand blessings to Corˢ Riordan
Juddy Riordan Jeffery and Thomas Prendergast.

4. From James Prendergast to his son Thomas

Mʳ Cornelius Riordan
Rear of No 8 Atkenson Street
Boston
America

Milltown July the 27ᵗʰ 1841

My Dear Thomas, I received your letter of 30ᵗʰ June last which
gave me ~~and~~ Mother and Brothers a good deal of pleasure
in finding ₍you₎ and the rest of the family in as perfect state
of health as this leaves me at present thanks be the
Lord. Now Danˡ Riordan is with Mʳ Finn at the Victoria
Hotel having only 1ˢ/6ᵈ per week hardly has much as keeps him
Tobacco. He was prepared to write to his brother some time
past and reserved one shilling to write but it happened to be
two sixpence piece and his step Mother took it away from him

---

4. The word has been blotted out, but may have been *Mother*.
5. The paper is damaged where the letter was sealed.

which detained him since of having written to ye long since. He
had a pair of shirts from a Gentleman in Killarney and he sent
them to one of his sisters to be washed but they said they
were stolen from them. I was speaking to him in Killarney a
few days ago and he is in the latter end of the clothes at present.
He is in perfect health at present. Your Brother Maurice intends
going to Curraglass or Glenflesk on the first of November next. Now
my Dear Child, I write you hoping you will be kind enough
in remitting me some money as soon as possible and but
having a particular and worthy friend at the helm which
you are aware of we would be backward as the rates got
pretty smart here this Summer in the latter end. The potatoes
were from 4ˢ/0ᵈ to 4ˢ/6ᵈ per peck and other sorts of food and nourishment
accordingly. Besides that fireing was doubly more expensive in this
Town as the Summer was very indifferent. I bought a pig which
cost me the sum of one pound ten shillings which I have
at present. I bought same out of your ˏlastˏ remittance. Dear Thomas
I hope you will let me know in your next ˏletterˏ how my Dear Judy
is situated also Cornelius Riordan her beloved husband as you
have not mentioned to me this time past how they were
situated and prospering in the world. I trust you will let
me know in your next letter. Mrs Fleming intends sailing
off on the next opportunity as she has the sum of thirty shillings
and expects to get a little more though going to Cork with John
Gnaw who promised her some money afterwards deceived her
and she spent a little there during her stay there in expectation
of being sailing with the above person but after all left her
at the see side. I dread ye may lose anything with John
Gnaw. Beware yourself of him. He behaved a great skeamer
in this country at his departure. He even went by night.
Without much trouble to yourself let me know if you should
know one William Keating who acted steward in the Navy Yard
in Boston or of two others (ie) a Nephew and Niece of the above person

who lives in Charleston[6]. She is married but we cannot know her
husbands name. If you should know said persons let me know.
Your Mother Brothers and friends join with me in
Love to you and Jeffeory Judy and not forgetting Cornelius
Riordan and remain your affectionate Father
until death.
James Prendergast
James Reordon got the
paper Con sint him
This is my wright
feare ye should think
Id be dead.
James Prendergast[7]

6. Charlestown, Massachusetts, now a neighborhood of Boston.
7. The postscript appears to be written in James's own hand.

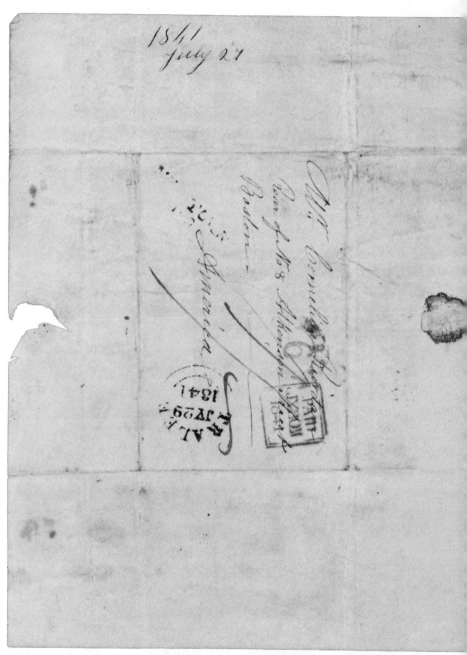

LETTER 4. Dictated to scrivener Patrick Mahoney by James Prendergast. It is typical of the letters in the collection, but it also includes a postscript written and signed by James himself.

Milltown July the 27th 1841

My Dear Thomas, I received your letter of 30th June last which gave me and Mother and Brothers a good deal of pleasure in finding you and the rest of the family in as perfect state of health as this leaves me at present thanks be the Lord, Now Danl Riordan is with Mr Finn at the Victoria Hotel having only 4/6 per week hardly as much as keeps him tobacco. he was prepared to write to his brother some time back and reserved one shilling to write but it happened to be two Six pence piece and his Step Mother took it away from him which detained him since of having written to ye long since he had a pair of Shoes from a gentleman in Killarney and he sent them to one of his Sisters to be washed but they said they were stolen from them. I was speaking to him in Killarney a few days ago. and he is in the latter end of the calathes at present he is in perfect health at present. Your Brother Maurice intends going to Curraglass or Glanflesk on the first of November next, Now My Dear Child, I write you hoping you will be kind enough in Remitting me some Money as soon as possible and but having a particular and worthy friend at the helm which you are aware of we would be backward as the rates got pretty smart here this Summer in the latter and the potatoes were from 4/0 to 5/6 per peck and other sorts of food and nourishment

Accordingly besides that firing was doubly more expensive in
Town as the Summer was very indifferent, I bought a pig wh
Cast me the Sum of one pound ten Shillings which I ha
at present I bought Same out of your last Remittance Dear I
I hope you will let me Know in your Next letter how my Dear
is Situated also Cornelius Riordan her beloved husband as
have not Mentioned to me this time past how they are
Situated and prospering in the world I trust you will
me Know in your Next letter, Mrs Fleming intends Saile
off on the Next opportunity as she has the Sum of thirty Shillin
and expects to get a little more though going to Cork with
Gnaw who promised her Some Money afterwards deceived
and she spent a little there during her stay there in h
of being Sailing with the above person but after all left h
at the Lee Side I dread ye May lose any thing with P
Gnaw beware yourself of him he behaved a great Skea
in this Country at his departure he even Went by Nig
Without Much trouble to yourself let me Know if you shou
Know one William Keating who acted Steward in the Navy
in Boston or of two others & c, a Nephew and Niece of the above
Who lives in Charleston she is Married but we cannot Know
husbands Name if you should Know said persons let me

Your Mother Brothers and friends Join with me in
Love to you and Jeffery Judy and not forgetting Cornelius
Jordan and Remain Your Affectionate Father
untill death.

         James Prendergist,

James Reordon got the
paper Con sent him
This is my weight
feare ye Should think
I'd be Dead

     James Prendergett

5. From James Prendergast to his children in Boston

M[r] Cornelius Riordan
Rear of No. 8 Atkinson street
Boston
America

Milltown September 29th 1841

My dear children, I received your letter of the 1st sep[t]
together with your remittance of five pounds sterling.
I feel thankful to you for your generous and kind
=hearted remittance now together with finding you and
each of you in as perfect state of health as this leaves
us[8] at present thank God for the many endowments
he has bestowed on us. Now my Dear children I intend
acquainting you respecting my health. I had been unwell
since the first of August last which I would not wish
acquainting you in my last letter, fearing you should
take my illness too much to heart. I am perfectly recovered
at present thank God. Now nothing seemed more disagreeable
to me and your beloved mother than hearing of Thomas's
sickness and knowing that the last letter was not written
by him added to our grief fearing he should be unwell.
Also a Killarney woman who came home lately acquainted
us that my Dear child Judy was not getting her health
in that country. Now I hope and trust at the arrival
of this letter you will send us an answer mentioning
the state of your healths not denying the verity of the
case. Daniel Riordan is still in the same situation

---

8. The word *us* is written over the crossed-out word *me*.

And is perfectly well in health but being as I have
mentioned in my last letter respecting his deficiency in
Cloathing at present. Mrs Fleming will precisely go to that
Country on the first of April next and your mother will
send nine pair of socks by her three pair of long stocking and
two pair for Judy. She would presently go but the disagreeableness
of the weather in this Country during the summer and what
is spent of harvest. The elders of the Country does not recollect
seeing such wet weather. Your Beloved Brother Maurice is
still in the same place at present. He does not know how long
he may continue it until the 1ˢᵗ of November next. Maurice
could not ₐknowₐ by any means that Richard Eagar Esqʳ was in
New york but he was in Dublin and also in England.
Roger Sheehy of Coolroe received a check of £6.0ˢ.0ᵈ stg.
Rathpogue is still in the Court of Equity. I do not know any
thing concerning it until March assizes. I expect you
will not give yourself any trouble to serve John Gnaw.
As you spoke in your letter about the postage I receive
your letters free always. Your Brothers and all their
families are well with all enquiring friends. Your Brother
John[,] Maurice and Michael join with us in love
to you and each of you. I remain your affectionate
and most devoted father until death.
James Prendergast

6. From James Prendergast to his son Thomas

Mr Cornelius Riordan
at the Rear of N° 8 Atkinson
street
Boston
America

Thomas Prendergast
Boston
America
Massachusetts

Milltown April the 28th 1842

My Dear Thomas, I take this favourable opportunity of
writing to you hoping to find you and the rest
of the family in as perfect state of health as this
leaves me and your affectionate mother and Brothers
and families at present thank God. I have sent
fifteen pair of stockings to you by John Quirk who left
this Town in this present month namely four pair of
light grey two of the pairs plainly knitted and two ribbed
two pair of socks of light Blue one plain and one ribbed two pair of
do⁹ grey ribbed one pair of white ribbed three pair of Black
worsted stocking plain. To my loving child Judy three pair
of long stockings ribbed one white one dark grey and one light
Blue together with plenty of thread along with each pair.
Dear Thomas your sister Judy can easily know these as
they were all knitted by your affectionate mother dreading

---

9. *Do* is an abbreviation of *ditto.*

any exchange being in their way. Dear Thomas we felt
very uneasy this time past as not getting an answer to the
last letter which was written in the month of February last
dreading any of you may be unwell in not writing to me
since. Your affectionate Brother Maurice has got a young
turn over
Daughter namely Judy. Daniel Riordan is well living in
the same place still. He was with us here not long since.
The Brothers and families are all well thank God.
Dear Thomas we had as severe a winter and spring
here as any man recollects seeing. We have within this
month most charming weather. Most wonderful business
has been done in this country within this month. As not
getting a fair spring you may judge provisions are
pretty smart here at present white lumpers from 3^{d} to 3½^{d} per
stone minions from 4^{d} to 4½^{d} per stone but we are in general
daily waiting for the Corn Bill being past that we may
expect cheap times particularly they expect having the
American flour over. I remain your affectionate and
humble Father until Death
James Prendergast
Bleachroad
P.S. I expect an answer to this as soon as possible as
we are uneasy this time past as not getting an answer
to the last.

. . . is America getting any improvement in the line of business as a great many of the neighbours who left this came home again.

JAMES PRENDERGAST,
August 1842

7. From James Prendergast to his children in Boston

Mr Cornelius Riordan
N° 22 Atkinson Street
Boston
America

Thom

Milltown August the 20th 1842

My beloved children, I received your letter of the 31st July last on the
15th of August Ins^t with your remittance of £5..0^s.0^d stg.
and also the remittance which ye were kind to send to me
on May last I have received also. Now Dear children I wrote
to ye two different letters. From the last letter I understand ye
received none of them of which I specified the description of
stockings and socks I had sent ye by John Quirk. I hope ye got
the same I sent you. Their specimen are as follows four pair of
socks grey two ribed and two plain three pair of black worsted stockings
for Jude two pair of dark ribbed worsted socks one pair of white
ribbed socks one do of light blew ribbed and one pair of light blew plain
three pair of long worsted one white ribbed one dark with a broad rib
and one light blew ribbed small. The thread of every sock and stocking
sewed to itself of their colour. My Dear and beloved children
your Brothers and families are all well in health and your
beloved mother and I also thanks be to the Redeemer. All the
trouble we felt was in not hearing from ye this time past
until the last letter I received gave us the greatest comfort and
pleasure to find you all in sound and perfect health as this
leaves us all at present thank God. Dear children Daniel
Riordan is well in health is still in the Victoria Hotel in Killarney

but specifies that he has neither money or clothes from them nor does not get it but the little which supports nature so far as food.
(Turn over)
Dear children, as you mentioned about Mrs Riordan I understand she is very low in means in the world. She was overjoyed when she heard that Robert made ye out. The Springs mentions that if they were over they would make out a situation for Robert as they mentioned to Mrs Riordan. I have nothing to communicate to you respecting Rathpogue. The Springs arrived safe here in July last. Let me know in your next letter what you think concerning them as they say they will go back in five or six weeks time, for all that they are daily going and not the nearer of going. Dear children I was speaking to Mary Donoghue at Garrett Lynch's and is highly surprised
     that
her loving husband Mich[l] Sullivan did not send her a letter since May last or remit her some money to ship off as not having as much as would take her across the Atlantic. Dear and beloved children from your mother the Springs at our enquiry respecting ye when do ye intend coming to the native Isle as we are always impatient to know they told me ye never would come to Ireland. Therefore if it be your intent remaining in America Dear children I hope you will send for me as ye ought to know that nothing earthly would give me greater comfort than to have my remains with each and every one of you stretched if it were as far again off. Dear children we have one comfort for the winter we have a good Reck of Turf[10] in the Garden what we were not possessed of last winter when we should dearly buy it. Also I have sufficient potatoes until christmas. For the little I sat this year they proved effectually good. This harvest we have as fine a sumur and harvest as yet as we had these twenty years and as promising. Dear and Beloved children, I am anxious to know what is Judy doing

---

10. A stack of peat for use as fuel for the household.

and how does she feel in health. Also let us know in your next
letter is America getting any improvement in the line of business
as a great many of the neighbours who left this came home again.
Let us know whether Mrs Fleming arrived safe as we have not heard
from her since she went as her parents arc very impatient in not
hearing of her arrival. No more at present from your affection͵ate͵
Father Mother and Brothers who join with us in love and
friendship for Cornelius Riordan Judy Jeffery and Thomas until
Death. James Prendergast
P.S The writer of this letter and our letters always his name
is Patrick Mahony of this town who is married to Daniel Connell
Teacher's sister begs of you to make strick enquiry respecting a cousin
of mine who lives in Boston in the Town. His name is Patrick
Moynihan Tailor by trade. He lately got married there to a daughter
of one Buckleys. Also Ellen Kerisk from Lisevane who lately came home
knew his wife and her family there. Should you meet with him I
    confidently
request of you to make every enqury of him whether he knows where my
Brother Cornelius Mahony is or is he living wherein I nor his beloved
mother did not hear from him since christmas last as we are in
Tears and daily trouble any intelligence had from the Tailor respecting my
brother you will be kind to communicate in your next letter or tell my
cousin the Tailor to write to me to Milltown directed to Pat^k D Mahony
Landsurveyor

8. From James Prendergast to his children in Boston

Mr Cornelius Riordan
N° 22 Atkinson street Boston
State of Mass
America

prepaid
Thomas Prendergast
Thoma
Milltown
Boston[11]

Milltown October the 11th 1842

My Dear children, I take this opportunity of writing
you these few lines hoping to find each of you
in as perfect health as this leaves me your affection‸ate‸
mother and Brothers with their families at present thank
God for his infinite mercy. I always received your
letters even the last directed to Jer^h Connor and which is
most grievous and surprising to me that ye had not
received any letter from me this time past and writing
frequently to ye. Dear children let me know in your
answer to this whether you received a letter bearing date
the 20th of August last as I mentioned the particulars of
the affairs in it. I always received your drafts the one
of May of £5..o^s.o^d and the other in Augt last of £5..o^s.o^d stg.
Now Dear children as not getting my letters I have changed
from Milltown post to the Killarney post dreading it may
be a neglect of theirs. Dear children I have sent four pair

---

11. *Thomas Prendergast* is written three times on the address leaf, along with *Thoma* two times, and the
words *Milltown* and *Boston* once each.

of long stockings one for each of you by Catharine and Anne
Spring now the Mrs Springs which sailed from Cork on the
8th of October Ins^t. I expect you will answer this at the receipt
of this as usual and send me a particular acc^t respecting
(Turn over)
The Springs and also let me know about Robert Riordan
or has he any employment or is he still with ye. As I am
anxious to know what my affectionate child Judy is doing
as you never mentioned to me what she was doing in
any of your letters. Dear children both your mother and I
was not in better health these twenty years past as we are
at present thank God th° it would be a happy circunstance
to each of you were we in our long home. Dear children from
the enquiry made by your mother of the Springs of your ever
coming home they had told her ye never would. Therefore
if it be not your wish coming home your affectionate mother
would be most anxious to be with ye on the first of May
next as she would be better pleased being and dying with
you than elsewhere. Let me know in your next letter how is
Mich^l Sullivan getting on or is he still in your neighbourhood.
His Wife Mary Donoghue was not able to go to him this season
but will on May next according to the account or encouragement
sent by her husband and she is surprised why he does not
write frequently to her. Daniel Riordan still in the Victoria
Hotel. He is well in health. Richard Eagar Esqr Attorney is
Dead. A few days before his death he had settled with your
affectionate Brother Maurice and he passed his note to him for £8.10^s
which he does not expect to receive a penny by him for ever.
Also The Revd John Quill formerly your p.p.[12] of Milltown
but lately of Liselton near Listowel where he died and being
Intered there the loving boys of milltown went and brought him

---

12. *p.p.* is an abbreviation of *parish priest.*

to be buried in the chapel in milltown according to his own
wish tho his own friends chosed to have him with his father and
mother he was taken from their bosom and brought to milltown
where there was a magnificient procession from the time the corps
left Tralee. The Town was all lighted by different persuasions
in honor of our long lamented ˄Clergyman˄. He was waked in the Chapel
and intered within the Chapel where we had the greatest concour[. . .] [13]
of people of different creeds at the Burial all in mourning f [. . .]
Loss of that talented p.p. Dear children do not forget [. . .]
to me about the last letter if you have rec^d it or not as the [. . .]
of this letter was present at the posting of it namely Pat^k D Mahony
soninlaw to Danl M Connell schoolmaster. No more at present
from your affectionate Father mother and Brothers who join
with me in Love and Friendship for Cornelius Riordan Judy
Riordan Jeffeory Prendergast and Thomas Prendergast together with the
conclusive blessing from your mother. James Prendergast
The writer of this letter and who is a particular friend of mine and always
writes my letters but my signature his name is Patrick Mahony of
      milltown.
He begs of you to enquire about a cousin of ~~mine~~ ˄his˄ who is in Boston.
      His name is
Patrick Moynihan Tailor. He got lately married to a daughter to one Danl
Buckley who lives in Broadstreet. If you discover him tell him that I
      begged
of him to write to me about my brother Cornelius Mahony who went to
      America
along with him if he rec^d any account from him. Let him know that I
      wrote to
him about a fortnight since whether rec^d or no. I remain your Truly Pat^k
      D. Mahony
Milltown Landsurveyor

---

13. The paper is damaged where the letter was sealed.

9. From James Prendergast to his children in Boston

M[r] Cornelius Riordan
No 22 Atkinson Street
Boston Mass
America

Thomas Prendergast [14]
Thom [15]

Milltown March the 21st 1843

My Dear and beloved children, I had received your
letter of the 28th of February last which gave us all the
greatest astonishment in your not getting the letter
which I wrote you on the 28th of December last immediately
after your remittance until the receipt of your last
where I discovered you did not receive it. But at the
receipt of the last we found the greatest pleasure
to find you were all in as perfect health as this
leaves us all at present thank be to providence.
Now Dear children about the letters sent by me to
you I cannot say where the mistake lies. There are
a great many complaining of the posts more particularly
of our home post which the generality of people are
charging them with as having the error at the side
with respect to letters sent to any part of America.
Therefore I will post this letter in Killarney post office

---

14. *Thomas Prendergast* is written on the address leaf, on what would have been the back of the folded letter.
15. *Thom* is written in the margin of the address.

and every other letter for the future. Dear children you ought
to know that it is no neglect of mine but the fraud
used by the posts that nothing earthly would us greater
than hearing from you weekly if it could be possibly
obtained. You may rest assured that it is no neglect of
mine that we think the day long when not hearing from you
all. Even about the time we considered having an answer to
the last letter sent by us there is not an hour but your
affectionate mother or I would be at the post, until
we received your last letter where we discovered you did
not receive it. Your affectionate Brothers and families
are all well. Your Brother Maurice has no place from
the 25th of march Ins[t]. He does not know as yet where
he may be employed as the Eagars of Curraglass went
down the Country where they were before which leaves
your affectionate Brother Maurice out of a Situation
at present. Robert Riordan has come home to Killarney
in october last, and he has not made any boast of
your kindness towards him when with ye though his
mother had told me when I was in Killarney that it was
ye spoiled him pampering him with every thing good.
Daniel Riordan is still in the same place and is
well in health and pretty well clad and clean.
Turn over
Dear children, I beg of you to beware of the Quirks to
be civil and strange to them. M[r] Spring and family
are all well and in your letters always I expect you
will speak largely of the Springs in America as it would
be wish of these at home that it would be said
that they were doing well and in great Situations.
The Ladies there sent home a letter a few days ago and
they spoke very largely of you all. My Dear children
I expect your answer to this as soon as possible and

that[16] to me as usual as I get your letters always and
I cannot conceive the fraud with respect to our letters to ye.
No more at present from your ever affectionate Father
mother and Brothers who join with love and friendship
for you all.

James Prendergast

P.S I hope you will not forget knowing or mentioning
in your next letter and know from Patrick Moynihan Tailor
whether he received any account from Cornelius Mahony
my particular friend Patrick Mahony of milltown Landsurveyor ˄Brother˄
or whether he came down to Boston to christmas with his
cousin Patt Moynihan as he promised. Do not neglect this as he
is a man I have a great wish for[17].

10. From James Prendergast to his son Thomas

Mr Cornelius Riordan
No 22 Atkinson Street
Boston Mass
America

a ship letter
prepaid

Milltown June the 12th 1843

My Dear Thomas, I have received your welcome and
Joyful letter of the 15th of May last with your draft for
£6..0^s..0 sterling and gave both I and your affectionate

---

16. The paper on which the word *that* was written has adhered to the wax seal on the letter. The paper
    is torn, but the word is legible.
17. "Have a great wish for" is an idiom meaning "have great respect for."

mother the most Joyful pleasure of finding you all
in as perfect health as this leaves us all at present
thanks be to the divine redeemer. Your Brothers and
Families are all well in health. Your affectionate Brother
Maurice is still at Glenflesk. He has no employment as
yet. He has stopped convenient to his garden this
year as having no employment at present. Daniel
Riordan is in the same place and Situation still and
is in very good health. My Dear Thomas I had received
a newspaper from you some time before the receipt of your
letter. Whether you post paid for it I am anxious to know
as I was charged 2^d for same. My Dear children I have
to communicate to you the state of uneasiness we were in
this time past when we discovered ye did not receive any
of the four letters I had written to you this time Back until
the last which I posted in Killarney office. Dear Thomas
(Turn over)
there must be some fraud in our home post. I strongly
suspect it is for the lucre of the shilling they delay the
letters in the post I have strongly on my mind to believe.
But in your letters there is no fraud I alway receive therefore
direct them as usual to milltown post for me. I will for the
future post my letters either in Killarney or Tralee as I have
experienced you dont get mine. Let me know whether John
Healy of Killarney wrote to Cornelius since as I gave him the
Directions the last time I was in Killarney according to your
directions. Dear Thomas let me know in your next letter
whether you all are for coming ˄home˄ or no as you mentioned in
Mary Donoghue's letter therefore your affectionate mother is
anxious to know. Mr Francis Spring and family are all
in prime good health. The day before we received a letter from
you Mr Spring rec^d a letter from America from his own family
there. Dear Thomas we were so uneasy that at the time of Towhy's

daughter going to America (Mrs McCarthy) your mother followed her to
Killarney with a letter to you by hand being so dispaired you would
not get any. Let me know in your next letter whether you got same.
Dear Thomas this summer is very indifferent wet all through, but
thank God very cheap times. The Best of Black mingins at 1^s/6^d per Peck
Pork at 3½^d per lb. My Dear children we have some nice hams of old
sound Bacon waiting your arrival home together with a good
Fat pig which will be fit for sticking after your arrival here.
Let us know in your next letter when do ye intend coming home.
Let me know is it any difference yourselves and Mrs McKenna had
    wherein
you dont mention her in your letter at any time as her father
is always inquiring of us and the Father is surprised the son
does not send him any assistance. The Repeal is making
the greatest progress in this country. Some of our Magistrates has
been superseded for attending the meetings. Some of them are
Resigning of their own accord sooner than give up the Repeal.
No more at present from your affectionate Father mother and
Brothers who join with ₐus inₐ love and friendship for Cor^s Riordan
Mrs Julia Riordan Jeffeory and Thomas Prendergast
James Prendergast
From your humble friend
Patrick D. Mahony and feel thankful and extremely obliged to you in
the kind exertions you have taken with respect to my Brother's
    information.
I shall for ever feel thankful after your advertisement[18] should you
    discover
any inteligence to write us a letter speedily. Also I will feel obliged to you
    by

---

18. In the July 8, 1843, *Pilot* a "missing friends" advertisement reads "Information wanted of Cornelius
    Mahony, a native of Killarney, county Kerry. A ago [*sic*] he was supposed to be about 150 miles from
    St. John, N.B, in a place called Breorton. Any information respecting him will be thankfully re-
    ceived by Thomas Prendergast, 22 Atkinson st, Boston, Ms."

giving my best love to My cousin Pat[k] Moynihan Tailor and family and
 let him know
that I am well in health thank God. I am yours Truly Pat[k] D Mahony
I send one newspaper
the Kerry Evening Post
Inform me whether ye
got same.[19]

11. From James Prendergast to his children in Boston

M[r] Cornelius Riordan
No 22 Atkinson Street
Mass Boston
America

I sent one paper[20]

Milltown August the 3rd 1843

My Dear children, I received your letter of the 14th
day of July which gave me your affectionate mother
Brothers and families the greatest pleasure in finding
you all in as pefect state of health as this leaves
us in general at present thanks be to providence.
Also I have received two Newspapers on the evening
of the 27th ultimo namely the New England reporter
but I discovered by your letter that you sent me three.
The third if sent I did not get. I made a charge on
the postmaster but he denyed getting same saying
that same did not leave America. Let me know

---

19. These four lines appear to have been written in a different hand from the main text of the letter.
20. This line is written in the margin of the address.

Francis Spring (1780–1868). Land agent for the Godfrey family of Milltown. (Photograph courtesy of Valerie Bary)

Father Bartholomew (Batt) O'Connor (1798–1890). Milltown parish priest from 1841 to 1886. (Photograph courtesy of Valerie Bary)

in your next letter. I had told them that you would
not mention same in your letter but sending it. I even
told them the name the Boston nation. Dear Thomas
I suspect strongly of a fraud in our home post
for the same evening your letter arrived your mother
was at the post office and asked for any commands, but
they denyed any being there. On the following morning
I called but I got your welcome letter. Daniel Riordan
is well in health and in the same place still. Also
Mr Spring and family are all well.
Turn over
Dear Thomas I mean letting you know that the post
in milltown is higly suspected for fraud even by
the generality of the people. I have instances of it myself
for lately any letter I posted there you did not get
until I went to Killarney postoffice. Therefore futurely
any letter having any remittance direct it to the
Reverend Bartholomew OConnor p.p milltown do not
speak of my name on the postscript, but any ˄other˄ letter
direct it to myself. Your Brother Maurice intended
writing to you. He has no situation at present. He has
stopped convenient to his Garden this season but is well
himself and family. Dear Thomas the times are not
troublesome as yet amongst us. We had some items on the
last news of the Orangemen[21] turning out in the north
against the catholicks but I tell you candidly that the
catholicks threshed them from right to left. Also they considered
the rufians of peelers and magistrates there to be partial to the
Friday flesh eaters. They the catholicks Bastardly pucked them
through and fro which is one of our victories. Nothing of any
importance we have not but that Bobby Peel gave us

---

21. Members of the Orange Order, a Protestant political society.

an arms Bill for Ireland. Repeal is carrying on in great
splendour in this country
by our Liberator Dan[l] OConnell M.P. We are all in
this country Repealers. The government are sending over
daily drafts of soldiers to Ireland but we defy them. We
are peaceable continuing our Repeal demonstrations all
through. Dear Thomas we were told that Mich[l] Roger Sheehy
got married in that country to Mrs Herbert formerly. Let me
know in your next letter. No more at present from your
affectionate Father mother and Brothers who join with ˄us˄ in
love and friendship for Cor[s] Riordan Julia Riordan Thomas
and Jeffeory Prendergast until death. James Pren[. . .][22]st
N.B From Patrick D. Mahoney Landsurveyor Milltown
Dear Sir, I am extremely thankful to you and ever will, in
the extraordinary trouble you have taken with respect to my
Beloved Brother. I may say that I give him up as dead in
not hearing from him going on his third year in that country.
If he was in S[t] John New Brunswick last year it is a mistery
where he is gone to since. I very harly believe same. As I am always
troublesome to you I expect you will tell my cousin Patrick Moynihan
to write to Dan[l] Morley or some friend to S[t] John seing would they
have any inteligence of him. When he wrote the place was Breton
not Breorton as mentioned in the paper. It is a cape as I have seen
in the Gazetteer. Dear Sir I Rec[d] two papers from you called the Boston
    Pilot
and am extremely ˄thankful˄ to you for your kind favours and shall never
    forget same.
Give my best love to my cousin Pat[k] moynihan and family. I am yours
    Pat[k] D Mah[. . .][23]
wishing to see him once more.

---

22. The paper is damaged where the letter was sealed.
23. The paper is damaged.

The only thing amongst us is agitation
for the Repeal of the union.

JAMES PRENDERGAST,
October, 1843

12. From James Prendergast to his son Thomas

Mr Cornelius Riordan
No 22 Atkinson Street
Mass Boston
America

a private ship letter

Milltown October the 13th 43

My Dear Thomas, I had received your letter of the
15th September last with your check of £5..0^s..0^d
stg. which gave us all the greatest pleasure of
finding you all in as perfect state of health
as this leaves me your affectionate mother Brothers
and their families at present thanks be to providence.
Dear Thomas I have to communicate to you that your
Brother Maurice had told me that David Murphy
of Killarney shopkeeper was telling him that he received
a letter from Cor^s Riordan from America and asked him
whether he had any thing to communicate to ye as
he was to write him an answer in a few days.
Your Brother Michael had Burried two children
namely Mary and James as ye were particular to know.
The eldest daughter lives namely Judy and a second
James. He has aged about twelve months a fine promising
Boy. Dear Jeffeory Miss Avice Spring begs of you to speak
to Catharine Spring otherwise Mrs Spring and that privately
she expects to hear from her so far as something
Turn over
of her kindness towards her aunt as being so far
from her. Therefore she begged of me to let you
know the same as she would depend on you beyond

any as you would be the only person to send any
thing had. Do not forget mentioning in your next letter
to me the answer you are made by Mrs Catharine Spring.
Dear Thomas please to inform Mrs McKenna that the money
sent home by Judy Sullivan Quart to her Father that the
mother got none of it therefore she expects you will speak
to Mrs Gnaw to advise the little girl in the next remittance
not to forget herself as she was surprised at the daughter
that she did not send her something according to promises.
Daniel Riordan is well in health and in the same situation
still in Killarney Hotel. Dear Thomas I hope you will not
trouble yourself futurely to the Revd Batt OConnor as he seemed
displeased at paying the postage. He paid o^s/6^d for the two papers.
Therefore dont trouble yourself in sending any papers to him.
Also Direct your letters futurely to myself as usual. I
expect you will send me a paper now and then as I will
not be displeased at paying the postage and write to me
as soon as possible. Turn over
Dear Thomas I mean informing you of the state of the
country. The rates are very indifferent that our country
Farmers are in a bad state through the depression of
prices. Even the most influential and wealthy Farmers
in your time in this country are very badly situated.
Trades of every description low nothing doing. The only thing
amongst us is agitation for the Repeal of the Union.
We are all Repealers in this country unless an
odd slow [24] as on the top of a tree in the month
of December (ie a few rotten members of poor
Palestines [25] and bigotted ones. Cor^s Prendergast pensioner [26] is

---

24. Sloe: the fruit of the blackthorn tree.
25. Palatines: a Protestant refugee group from Germany, some of whom settled in Ireland in the eighteenth century.
26. A former member of the military who collected a pension.

Dead and burried since Sunday last the 8th Inst. No more
at present from your affectionate Father mother and Brothers
who join with us in love and friendship for Cors Riordan
Judy Riordan Jeffeory and Thomas Prendergast until death.
James Prendergast
From Patrick Mahoney
Dear Sir, I cannot convey words sufficient to
denote the obligation I am under to you in the extreme trouble you had
taken with respect to my Brother but this alone that I wish you all and
every day's prosperity and long life. I must give him over as dead. Please
to remember me to my cousin Patk Moynihan. I am yours Truly Patk
    Mahony

13. From Michael Prendergast to his brothers Jeffrey and Thomas

Mr Cornelius Riordan
No 22 Atkinson Street
Boston Mass
America
to be forwarded to Mr Jeffeory
Prendergast

prepaid

Milltown November the 3rd 1843

Dear Brothers, I take this first opportunity of
addressing you hoping to find you all in general
in as good health as this leaves me and family
with my affectionate Father and mother at present
thanks be to providence. Dear Brothers I intend

troubling you a little. As being my first request and
I trust as faithful subjects and Brothers you will not fail
sending same (ie) the sum of £3..0^s.0^d. By remitting
me this to purchase a mule would be the greatest
means of making me comfortable through life.
At sending for this to you Dear and affectionate
Brothers I did not acquaint my Father or mother of it.
I would be capable of getting through life well enough
but meeting with disappointments these two years
past with regard of being unwell myself that left
me deficient of money at present. Therefore if you
remit me the above sum it will flourish me through
life moreover as I got well in health thank God for his
gracious gifts. (Turn over)
And should you send me same if ever you should
come to Ireland again if I had no other way of paying
you but giving up same I will pay you. Therefore as
being the first I expect you both will not fail to send
me the sum of £1..10^s each which will be the greatest
means of sustenance for me and family. Therefore do
not fail to write to me speedily as I would have to
write again and again until I receive your answer
as I thought at our last fairwell inside the ditch
of the old Pike near Killarney that I would not be so
long from seeing you. Dear Brothers Jeremiah Sheehan
Kate White's son being with Sir Wm Godfrey Bar^t as
servant he and one McDonnell this McDonnell and
he made an attempt of robbing Sir W^{ms} desk of money
of which they were in Bridewell these days past until
Sheehan being bailed by James Godfrey. McDonnell has
gone to jail to stand his Trial at the coming assizes
and also Sheehan. Transportation is sure to them. They
had false keys and found on MDonnell's person.

Dear Brothers the times are very dul in this country
Rates very low and no employment for labourers.
Repeal carried on on the greatest terms.
Dan¹ OConnell was arrested in Dublin he and a great
many of the nobility to stand their trial on the
6ᵗʰ Insᵗ but we hope that the trial will be of no
avail. Dear Brothers two of my children died last
year as I may say one on to day and one on the
following day. No more at present from your
affectionate Brother wishing you Thomas and Jeffeory
Prendergast not forgetting my loving Sister Judy and her
loving husband Corˢ Riordan every happiness and
Remain for ever until Death your
loving Brother
Michael Prendergast
P.S
Let Corˢ Riordan and Judy know that I have sent for
this trifling sum. Direct the letter to my Father
when you are remitting any to him who will give
me the above sum if you send it for me to him.
If you are sending it mention it for me in your
letter and he will give it to me safely.
MP
My Fatherinlaw and I does not chime well. What he promised
me I did not get which was one of the disappointments.

14. From James Prendergast to his son Thomas

Mr Cornelius Riordan
No 22 Atkinson Street
Boston Mass
America

prepaid

Milltown December the 3rd 1843

My Dear Thomas, I received your letter of the 14th November
on Sunday morning the 3rd Inst which I write you this
Immediately but I received not papers as yet ₐnor Father Battₐ if we dont
hereafter, but the former papers you sent Father Batt.
I had written you a letter in answer to Jeffeorys letter
on the 14th of October last together with a paper of our
Receipt of his check of £5..0s.0d stg. I find no
difficulty in Tralee in Cashing your checks. I only
send it into the Tralee Bank and in nine days I get
the full amount. Now Dear Thomas we felt the greatest
pleasure Immaginable of hearing that ye were all in as
perfect health as this leaves me your affectionate mother
Brothers and families at present thanks be to providence.
Your Brother Maurice is still in Glenflesk but in no
situation as yet. Danl Riordan is very well and in the
same situation and is very comfortably clad. The
friends and neighbours are all well. The last letter sent
you of the 14th October last contained many important
new which I expect you will receive the same letter before
this. I received Jeffeory's draft of the 15th September last.
From your affectionate mother who begs of you to let her

know in your next letter what Judy is doing and is
she in perfect health and also Cor^s Riordan in good health.
No more at present from your affectionate Father
~~and~~ mother and Brothers who join with me in love and friendship
for Cor^s Riordan Judy Riordan Jeffeory and Thomas Prendergast
until death, &c.

James Prendergast

N.B Danl O'Connell the Liberator was on his trial in
Dublin this time past for treason against the government
(ie) for holding repeal meetings for enticting the people
at those meetings and for introducing arbitration Courts
in Ireland and also for collecting money at home and from
foreign Lands called America they say for the dismember
=ment of the Empire but, they are liers. Danl means no
such thing. He means equal laws eq^l justice and equal Right
to Ireland together with some means of support for the
poor of all Ireland. He has beaten them upon their clauses.
The Trial was adjourned until the 15th of January next
which it is supposed will never be called.
There is a great tribute making up for the Liberator
now thro Ireland. It is computed to be about £40,000 stg.
From Pat^k D Mahoney I hope you will remember me
to my cousin Patt Moynihan and family and give them
my blessing.

15. From James Prendergast to his children in Boston

To Mr Corneilus Riordan
N° 22 Atkinsons
Street Mass
Boston
America

Bleach road Milltown Feby 27th 44

Dear children,
Through this post office I received your
letter directed to my son Michael which letter I
had no knowledge of or that he ever wrote to ye
and indeed he had no occasion to apply in
that kind of way for he is very comfortable at
home. I received that much information by open
ing his letter for he never told me that he
wrote to you. I am glad thro that that ye
all enjoy a good share of health as we do
thanks be to god. Still at the same time
I do not intend to put any hindrance that
ye may send him what ye please tho he
has no need of it. Be assured I frequently
answered your letters and my reason for coming
by his letter thinking it may be directed to
him as it was to Jerry Connor Publican of
this town as ye may think that old age
may have sent us to our graves. Dear
children I received three letters from you one
dated

dated September 15th 1843 one November 14th 43
and the other November 30th of which I answered.
I now beg to inform you that each of your
money letters cost me some trouble except
the order on the Tralee bank I had no trouble
or expense. I hope Dear children that ye have
no blame to me. I always answered each of your
letters and I would be glad to know if ye received any
of them or not that I may know from the general
post office of this kingdom what became of them.
So I expect that on receipt of this letter write
to me as quick as possible. There is one thing I
expect that any more letters written by this Patt
Mahony will not be answered; with his constant
trash about his friend over, for he played a great
trick in advising my son to trouble you contrary to
my knowledge when he had no need. I can
tell you whenever this Mahony wrote for me I paid
very well therefore I am under no compliment to
the poor pedagogue. I can inform you that
John Quart received 6£ from his daughter.
I can also inform you fearing that some
fraud might be practiced regarding those letters
I changed in putting this letter in Milltown post
of office that it may arrive with ye into
the killarny post office. In Futher direct
your letter to your Father and send no
news papers to his Reverence.
I have to inform you
that John Thos Eagar died in the north
and Rathpogue is now in the hands
of the Godfrey family.

I remain your attached
and loving Father
Juliana Pendergast
and Con Riordan your husband
likwise Jeffry and Thomas
James Prenderg₍ₐ₎as₍₎[27]

16. From James Prendergast to his children in Boston

Mr Cornelius Riordan
N° 22 Atkinson Street
Boston State of Mass
America

Milltown May the 24th 1844

My Dear Children, I have to address you with
these few lines hoping to find ye all in general
in as perfect state of health as this leaves me
your affectionate mother Brothers and their families
at present thanks to providence. Dear Jeffeory I
have to acquaint you that I received your letter of
the 30th of April last with your check of £5..0^s.0^d stg.
which I was obliged to send to Dublin and had lost
one shilling postage and to the 3 or 4 checks sent me
this time past except the check which you had sent
about christmas last which I got in Tralee. Therefore if
you should draw on the Bank of Ireland Tralee
payable to me I would get the money the very day of

---

27. James runs out of space for his signature.

my going to Tralee as is most natural from years and
Infirmity that I cannot be very strong. Dear Jeffeory I
have to acquaint you that your Bother Maurice and
family is living in the Town of milltown. He is jobing
in pigs and cattle with the little money reserved by him
and for this year he is sowing a good Garden. Since he
left his situation your Brother John and family are
well but in low circumstances. He has left the situation
which he held in Tralee. Since the death of Mr Charles
Agar he had no quarters by them worth mentioning.
Therefore he had left them at christmas last but he
had left them of his own free will without blemish
and on as good terms as ever they were. Dear Jeffeorey
your Brother Michael and family are well in health and
the Trifle which he sent for ∧to∧ ye I expect if you possibly can
to remit him same to purchase a little mule as he represents
he would live comfortable had he the mule as he blames
me for the money not coming. Since he received your letter
there were four sheep killed and stolen from him in his
own field. The heads and trotters he found after the night
in the field with young lambs in them. I say that he would
be capable of pulling out were not for that occurrence.
Dear Jeffeory I have to acquaint you that Doctor Agar has
gone to the East Indies and has got a Beautiful situation
as head Doctor in an Establishment and his Brother
Rowland Agar went in two months after the Doctor in a
place called Solone[28] in the East. Dear Jeffeory you will
be pleased to let Mrs McKenna know that her father
Roger Sheehy is dead these two months past and as I was
Informed Died in poverty though having money in Bank by
the wife and from what I could see I could suspect no

---

28. *Solone* is Ceylon, now Sri Lanka.

Better. The coffin which was around him was more like
a county coffin falling asunder at conveying him to his
natural Burying place. Dear Jeffeory I have to acquaint
you that your affectionate mother had sent four pair of
stockings to Judy Riordan by Margaret Fitzgerald. They
were marked for her. The colour two grey pairs one Black and
one white 3 pair ribed and one plain. Dear Jeffeory I have
to acquaint you of a young man who left this country lately
namely Jerry Sheehan who was as coachman to Sir W^m
D. Godfrey Bar^t had been discharged from that situation
by reason of some money being stolen from Sir W^m D G Bar^t.
He and a Boy that was in the house as servant name[. . .] [29]
[. . .] [30] McDonnell which McDonnell was Transported [. . .]
15 years. Sir W^m did not prosecute. Jerry Sheehan would have
met with the same fate if prosecuted. Therefore I counsel ye to
beware of him. Keep yourselves civil and strange to him
the Report being that he was as guilty as the other if prosecuted.
Let me know in your next letter how John Ford is getting on
and how is his Eye. We have a parching summer here this
summer. Pat^k Mahoney begs of you to remember him to his cousin
Pat^k Moynihan and family. I conclude my letter by wishing you every
          hapiness
with your affectionate mother Brothers and families who join with me in
love to Cor^s Riordan Judy Riordan Jeffeory and Thomas Prendergast
until Death. Write to me as soon as possible.
Let me know how is Cor^s Riordan at
present situated or has he any place
at present.
James Prendergas‸t‸

29. The paper is damaged where the letter was sealed.
30. McDonnell's first name appears to be John.

17. From James Prendergast to his children in Boston

Mr Cornelius Riordan
Boston N° 22 Atkinsonstreet Mass
North America

T.S.P.

Milltown 18th July 1844

My Dear Children
On the 15th Instant I received Thomas' Letter of the 30th of
June last. It was to me a precious gift. Nothing could give me
and your Mother so much pleasure as an assurance that ye
all are well. It is the subject of our prayer, night and morning,
that the Lord may pour his blessings on you and continue his
favours to you. Your Mother and I are well thank God and so
are your Brothers Maurice and Michael and their respective fa
=milies. Daniel Riordan is well in health but looks poorly for
want of clothes. He is still at Finn's Hotel in Killarney. I went there
last week in order to see him. He told me that he had plenty
to eat and drink but that he got only 15^s last season and that
had no promise of wages this season. I requested of him
to come home with me and that I would buy a coat and Trowsers
for him, but he would not. He said that Con would send it
to him at some time. He said he was really offended when Con
wrote to David Murphy and never enquired about himself.
He begged of me ˄to˄ state this to Con. Mrs Riordan and family
are well in health but only middling in other respects. M^{rs}
(James Robin) Eagar died in Killarney some time
since.
I am really glad to hear that Larry and his Brother are well and

that John is getting better daily. I hope Larry has got a good
match and may god bless them. Their Mother is in Cork and
I am told by some of those carmen that see her that she looks very
poorly. She sent to me repeatedly to know where her sons were. She
complains that they never wrote to her or enquired how she was.
Tell them that she is very poorly situated and that I am
credibly informed it would be much better and easier
for her to be among her neighbours here than where she is.
At least that if she had one or two Pounds to buy little
light articles of traffic she could do much better. Speak
to them and let them know the entire matter. It would do them
credit if they sent her a trifle. It it would be infinite service
to her while they could scarcely feel it. We have no local
news of any interest here at present. As the Writ of Error upon
the state Trials is still in the Lords and the issue not yet
known here. All other news is disregarded here. Every
liberal asks for no other than that upon which depends the
freedom or continued incarceration of the Liberator and his
fellow suffering Patriots. The greatest anxiety prevails and
the issue most impatiently looked for. A few days must determine.
I should not forget your Brother John (Want of good nature
was not his fault) He and his family are well in health. He lives
in Tralee. Provisions were not dear with us this year but
great fears are entertained regarding the next as many are
complaining of failures in their sowings this year,
but God alone can dispose of future Events.
Your Mother feels hurt at desiring her to send no more
stockings. She says she would feel a pleasure in
knitting them for ye. She joins with me in sending
you our love and blessing and I remain your
affectionate Father
James Prendergast

P.S.

Mr Spring and every member of his family are perfectly
well. I would say more about them and they would not
be last but I am sure Mr Spring has answered the
letter which he received when Thomas' Letter
arrived with me.

18. From James Prendergast to his children in Boston

Mr Cornelius Riordan
No 22 Atkinson Street
Boston Mass
America

Milltown November the 9th 1844

Dear children, I Anticipate the receipt of your
loving and welcome letter with your check of £5..0^s.0^d
stg. and I feel extremely and parentially thankful
in your remittances at all times. I am Dear children
Informed that it is very hard Earned. Therefore
I have to give you in Lieu thereof both mine and
your affectionate mother's many Blessings together
with finding you and all of you in as good health
as this leaves me your affectionate mother Brothers and
their families at present thanks to Providence.
Dear Thomas I have to acquaint you with respect
to our going to that Country. Should ye be inclined
to remain in that country it would be our wish to
be stretched along side ye wherever ye should be, but

were ye to come home to the native Isle or if it be
your wish why we should like to be intered with the
Forefathers. Dear children we leave all at your own
disposal. You ought to know that nothing would give me
greater pleasure than being where you would be.
As for the Repeal which you have spoken of in your letter
it is a wise man can foretell. But were we to die on the
voyage were it the will of Providence we would be content
and being where your remains would be. Therefore act
as your genius leads you. Dear Thomas Mrs Spring
begs of Jeffeory in his next letter to let her know about
her daughters and families as she received no letter from
them these three months tho being writing continually.
She does not know whether they received any of her
letters. Dear Thomas I wrote to your aunt Catharine Ford
to Cork and she is well inclined to go and also her
soninlaw John Barry and family if her children should
Encourage them. Dear Thomas let Cor^s Riordan know that
his Brother Danl Riordan is still in the same situation
in the Victoria Hotel Killarney and is well in health.
Beware of John Flynn of the Abbey which I am informed
is in Boston. He is what we commonly call a trickey.
Your Brothers namely Maurice John and Michael and their
families are well in health. If you could conveniently
draw upon any of the Tralee Banks I would not be
under the necessity of sending to Dublin and paying
a shilling postage together with the delay attending
same in going to Dublin. The writer of this letter
namely Patrick D. Mahoney Landsurveyor Milltown I was
Informed about a month ago by a young woman of
the name of Judy Moynihan that my Brother Cor^s
Mahoney was lately come to the vicinity of Boston.
My cousin Patt Moynihan knows Judy Moynihan. She

stopped with him for some time. I am putting you to
too much trouble about him but any inteligence
I will feel extremely thankful. I remain your
affectionate Father Mother and Brothers who join
with me in love a friendship to Cor⁵ Riordan Judy
Riordan Jeffeory and Thomas Prendergast unil Death
James Prendergast
I received your paper the Boston Pilot also I expect
your letter as soon as possible as we are most anxious
to hear from ye often, as the receipt of your letter is
at the lower calculation a twelve month younger to us
in place of getting old.

19. From James Prendergast to his son Thomas

Mʳ Cornelius Riordan
No 22 Atkinson Street
Boston Mass
America
December 6ᵗʰ 1844[31]

Milltown December the 6ᵗʰ 1844

My Dear Thomas, I received your welcome letter
of the 15ᵗʰ November last which gave me, your affection‸ate‸
mother ~~and~~ Brothers and their families the greatest
pleasure of finding you all in as good health as
this leaves me your beloved mother Brothers and families
at present thanks to Divine providence for all his

31. This date and an illegible word are written on what would have been the back of the folded letter.

Graces. Dear Thomas you alledge great blame to me
about my neglect in writing. I always write to ye regularly
and speedily whatever may be the delay in the offices.
I even sent ye a letter on the 20th of November last in which
all matters relative to our being well and the reception
of your check of £5..0[s].0[d] stg. was mentioned in same.
Dear Thomas, you speak of death being amongst us.
We have no case of the kind thank God. I and your
Beloved mother are well and strongly living still, tho
in truth we would have died long since by all reason
were it not for ye Dear children that are nourishing us
in our old and feeble days. May God thr° his infinite
graces give you all the greatest comfort and happiness.
Dear Thomas I expect we will live untill we enjoy that
one comfort of seeing you all together at Home.
(Turn over)
Dear Thomas, I beg of you to let me know in your next
letter to whom did you leave the Box which you got from
your Brother John at leaving the country as a few nights
ago some difference arose between your Brother John and Mich[l]
about the Box John having seen the key of the Box with
Mich[l] he said that the key was the actual key of the
Box which he gave you at your departure. Mich[l] denied
it. Therefore to quell all disunion let me know to
whom did you leave the Box. About your ages your
Brother Jeffeory's age being 28 years the 27th of May last
your own age being 25 years the 29th of last May.[32] Dear
Thomas we are most anxious to know your anx ̬c ̬iety for
your ages as we cannot conceive the reason therefore
let me know in your next letter. Dear Thomas Daniel
Riordan is well in health and in the same situation

---

32. James answers the question of Jeffrey and Thomas's birthdates again in each of the following two
    letters, giving a slightly different answer each time.

still in the Victoria Hotel Killarney. Dear Thomas it
me the greatest pleasure of hearing the Fords being well
and doing well. Your Aunt Kate is perfectly satisfied
to go to that country if she is sent for as I got a letter
from her from Cork some time past. Mr Spring and family
are all well in health. Dear Thomas about the Repeal
the Liberator Dan[l] ᴼConnell and his associates say that we
will actually have the Repeal tho in truth it is dangerous
Because there are some of our Irish for the Repeal
others for Federal Parliament therefore it is doubtful
what time we will have it as they are not alltogether
for the repeal. If they were we certainly would have
it and no mistake. No more at present from your
affectionate Father mother and Brothers who join
with me in love and friendship to Cornelius Riordan
Julia Riordan Jeffeory and Thomas Prendergast until
Death. James Prendergast

I am as well pleased as if he were at home hearing he is alive.

PATRICK MAHONY,
January 1845

20. From James Prendergast to his son Jeffrey

Mr Cornelius Riordan
No 22 Atkinson Street
Boston Mass
America

Milltown January the 17th 45

My Dear Jeffeory[33], I take this favourable opportunity
of addressing you and communicating to you the
Receipt of your last letter of the 1st of January Ins^t
with your check of £5..0^s.0^d stg. which I feel and
your affectionate mother extremely delighted of finding
you your lovely Brother Sister Judy Riordan and Cor^s Riordan
in as good health as this leaves me[,] your affectionate
mother Brothers and their families at present thank
God. Dear Jeffeory[34] all the letters I have Rec^d from
you since October last was as follows one on 15th October
the second on the 15th November and the last of the 1st
January Ins^t. I sent you an answer to all those letters
which I understand you did not Receive a letter which
I sent you dated November the 6th and posted in milltown.
And about your ages which you mentioned to me to send
you it was mentioned in the last letter of the 6th Nov^r.
Dreading you might not get the letter your ages are as
follows Jeffeorys age 27 years the 7th of May last and Thomas
25 years the 29th of May last. I and your mother were most
anxious to know your reason for your ages. Let us know in
your next. Dear Jeffeory we were highly surprised that
you did not mention in your last letters any thing

---

33. The name *Jeffeory* has been written over the name *Thomas*.
34. The name *Jeffeory* has been written over the name *Thomas*.

Respecting Cor^s Riordan or Judy. What are they doing or
is Cor^s Riordan at Home at present. Daniel Riordan
is well in health and in the same situation still
in the Victoria Hotel Killarney. Dear Jeffeory the check
which you sent me was not payable until thirty days after
date. I being so uneasy in writing to ye immediately that
I was not paid as yet. I will send you a correct account
about the payment of the check in my next letter.
Now Dear Jeffeory if you rec^d the letter of the 6th November
observe whether on the outside of it was mentioned ship
letter which Palmer wrote on the outside. Let me know
in your next if you got same. Dear Jeffeory ye seemingly
are uneasy about writing to ye oftener. I and your loving
mother are doubly uneasy in your negligence. Behold it
is not for wish of money because it would be a happy day
for ye we were in our long Home, but solely for love
for your persons. My Dear children I expect your answer
to this letter as soon as possible. Dear Jeffeory about the
Repeal. I cannot say much about it. We are mute at
present until the next sitting. We are much grieved
about a Bill which the Tories intend bringing into the House
the Bequest Bill [35] which we Trust they will be defeated.
They intend pentioning off our clergymen which if that
takes place will precisely put an end to Repeal. I
have no more to say at present but wishing you
your Brother Thomas Cor^s Riordan and Judy Riordan every blessing
together with wishing you all a happy newyear with your
affectionate mother Brothers and their families who join
with me in love and friendship to you all. [. . .] [36]
Remain your affectionate Father until Death.
James Prendergst

---

35. *Bequest Bill* refers to the Charitable Bequests Act of 1844.
36. The paper is damaged where the letter was sealed.

James FitzGerald begs of you Jeffeorey to have an eye after his
    daught[. . .]³⁷
Margaret who lately went to mention in your letter about her how she
getting through life as she depends on you particularly.
From Patᵏ D Mahoney. Dear Sir I am extremely thankful
to ye in the trouble you have taken in the information of
my Brother Cornelius. I am as well pleased as if he were at
Home hearing he is alive. There is one Daniel Morley
carpenter in Sᵗ John N.B which my cousin Patt Moynihan
knows where he lives. He might have seen him lately if Patt
Moynihan wrote to Morley. I beg of him to write to Sᵗ John.
I remain yours truly &c. Patᵏ D Mahoney

21. From James Prendergast to his son Jeffrey

Mʳ Cornelius Riordan
No 22 Atkinson Street
Boston Mass
America

Milltown March the 7ᵗʰ, 45

My Dear Jeffeory³⁸, I take this favourable opportunity
of addressing you hoping to find you all in
as good health as this leaves me your affectionate
mother Brothers and their families at present
thanks to Divine Providence, also of acknowledging
the Receipt of your last letter ₐof the 1ˢᵗ Januaryₐ with your remittance

---

37. The writer runs out of space.
38. The name *Jeffeory* is written over another word which has been obscured, but may be *Thomas*.

of £5..0ˢ..0ᵈ stg. Dear Jeffeory[39] I have to inform you that
I sent you two letters one on the 6ᵗʰ of December last
posted in milltown another on the 22ⁿᵈ January last posted
in Tralee. Whether ye got either I cannot say. You mention‸d‸
about the check whether we would get the amount
in Tralee. I freely got the amount, even before it was
payable. Dear Jeffeory I feel very uneasy as not getting
our letters regularly you may rest assured that it
is no neglect of mine that nothing earthly would give
me greater pleasure than hearing from ye often. Now
as you had mentioned in one of your letters to me about
your ages thᵒ mentioning your ages in the last two letters
sent ye dreading not getting either Jeffeory's age being
28 years the 7ᵗʰ of May next Thomas's age 25 years the 29ᵗʰ of May
next.
Turn over
Dear Jeffeory I cannot conceive the reason of your
Inquiry about your ages. I and your affectionate mother
is most anxious to know. Mention to me in your next
letter. Daniel Riordan is well in health and in the same
situation still in the Victoria Hotel Killarney.
Mʳ Spring and family are well. Dear Jeffeory I have
to inform you that your Brother Michael was preparing
to go to that yankey country until I and your beloved
mother prevailed on him to remain at home for this year
whatever may the consequence. The poor man has met
with many disappointments these late years and to
add to his trouble about a three weeks ago he had a
good ass the best animal that was ever handled and
which was the poor Boy's sole support. She died thrᵒ
the means of some Blackguards illtreating the poor animal.

---

39. The name *Jeffeory* is written over another word which has been obscured, but may be *Thomas*.

Now th° small an animal an ass is it was the greatest
loss to the Poor Boy in the commencement of spring. I
felt so much at his loss that I went to his Fatherinlaw
and had told him to give your Brother Mich¹ as much
as 12ˢ and that I would give him 12ˢ more to purchase
some kind of a little animal for him to aid him a little.
The Fatherinlaw declined giving a penny piece, therefore he
nearly despaired. He said that whatever may the consequence
that he would go and seek for fortune. Dear Jeffeory
your affectionate mother and I prevailed on him to remain
this year whatever. We thought it mournful being living
next door to us to have him leave the country. No more
to say but wishing you all every happiness and your
Brothers and mother who join with me in love and friendship
to Corˢ Riordan Judy Riordan Thomas and Jeffeory Prendergast
until Death and Remain your affectionate Father
James Prendergast
Write to me as soon as
possible and at the receipt
of this letter as I am
impatiently waiting your
letter.
From Patrick D Mahoney the last letter which I mentioned
to you about my Brother I was lately informed that it
was in a place called woodstock he was when lately
seen. I am very delicate in Troubling you as I am at all
times and if ever we should meet I never shall forget your
kindness. I Remain yours Truly Patrick D Mahoney

22. From James Prendergast to his son Thomas

Mr Cornelius Riordan
No 22 Atkinson Street
Boston State of Mass
America

prepaid
T.S.P.

Milltown[40] May the 21st 45

My Dear Thomas, I have to acknowledge the Receipt
of your welcome letter of the 1st Ins^t ‸on the 16th Ins^t‸ with your check
of £5..0^s..0^d stg. which gave me your affectionate mother
Brothers and their families the warmest pleasure of
finding you all in as perfect state of health as this leaves
me your affectionate mother Brothers and families at
present thanks to providence for his divine mercies.
Dear Thomas I have to acquaint you that I received
the amount of the check in the Tralee Bank
Immediately and receiving your letter if empty would
be as welcome to me [and] your affectionate mother as if it
contained £50 British. We were so impatient this time
past for not receiving a letter from ye we were doubtless‸ly‸
In dread something was the matter with one or either of you.
Dear Thomas you mentioned in your last letter the Receipt
of a letter the 9th of November last. You must have mistaken
the date. The last letter I wrote you was dated the 6th of
March last. Whether you received same I cannot say.
Dear Thomas I am always acquainted writing to ye regularly

----

40. The word *Milltown* is written over the word *May*.

if you receive them as I and your loving mother think a
month a year when we dont hear from you all. Moreover
our scriviner or writer ˄Patt Mahoney˄ is as free to us as if one of
      yourselves
were at Home. Therefore do not neglect writing to us
often, as it is my chief object. Tho we are a Burthen
on ye I well know it would be a consolation to ye
to hear from us. I know it from my own Bosom
as we get many years younger when we receive your
letter. Therefore do not neglect writing Immediately. Dear
Thomas I have to acquaint you that Daniel Riordan
is well in health and in the same situation still in the
Victoria hotel Killarney. Dear Thomas let me know in your
next letter how is James John and Laurence Ford and how
are they getting on. Dear Thomas your Brother Michael
seemed as much delighted at your letter with respect
to the little donation which ye intend sending as if he
had same in his Pocket he being so certain of your
Punctuality that he expressed he was sure now of same.
He wants a little horse badly and I am very glad you
did not encourage him to go to that country as he seems
not sound in health tho not having any sickness. I have
no more to say but wishing you all every happiness
with your Beloved mother Brothers and their families who join
with me in love and friendship to Corˢ Riordan Judy Riordan
Jeffeory and Thomas Prendergast and Remain your affectionate
until death.
James Prendergast
I expect an answer to this immediately.
From Jeremiah Connor of milltown Publican begs of you
to let him know in your next letter whether that
Country would be ˄a˄ good place for him to send his
Eldest son namely Patt Connor to. He is seventeen years

of age and is a proper honest Boy and a very
Proficient scholar. If ye could make out any situation
for him in a shop or otherwise to bind him to some
good trade for a few years as I am informed that in
that country they have a yearly salary together with
showing them their trade. Therefore as you consider the
best mode for him to have a clean livelihood I would
be most anxious to send him to that Country according
to the encouragement had from you in your next letter
and by your exertion in the above case I will for ever
be under the greatest obligation to you all. I having
seven in family that I would be most anxious to have
the eldest Boy in some good way to get thr° life than
have him in this miserable country in Poverty. No more
at present from yours Truly
Jeremiah Connor

23. From James Prendergast to his children in Boston

Mr Cornelius Reardon N° 2
Shortstreet Court Boston
state of Massachusetts
N. America

Pre-paid

Milltown 9th August 1845

My dear Children
On the 2nd of August Instant I received your Letter of the 15th
of last month. That I was happy to find ye were well is no more than

what every man must be, on hearing from his friend. To say this would
be [. . .]⁴¹ saying only what every man in my situation should say
but I have cause to be more joyful than others. I find that ye
are happy where so many suffer hardships. Also we were very uneasy
this time past. Your mother and I had so many dreams about
ye. We dreaded that something was the matter with you
but we are relieved from our fears, and we rest happy
in the assurance that ye are well. We are well in health, thank
God, and so are your Brothers and their families. Your Brother
Mich¹ desires to send ye his blessing, and his sincere thanks for
the kind promise ye made him. He certainly does not enjoy
good health, and certainly is not able to work well. If he had a
little Horse or Mule He says he could do, and that your promise will
enable him to get one. If ye see either of ₍your₎ Cousins the Fords, tell
them that their Mother is really distressed in Cork. Thoˢ Kelliher
the Carman told me he met her, worn and old and going about attempt
=ing to work for her daughters. She said that she was
very poorly situated endeavouring to work and unable to
do so. She said that she had not the sign of a cloak and
that if she had she would return to Milltown that
she could live more comfortably by begging among her
neighbours than she did where she was. Maurice
removed on the first July last. He lives with Mʳ John Lynch
at Dromin near Killarney. He has a very good place with
constant employment. His Wages are a House and Garden the grass of
a Cow, three sheep and his ass and six Pounds yearly. Nothing
troubles us except when we are for any length of time without
receiving an account from ye. Your Mother unites with
me in sending ye our love and blessing and I remain
your affectionate Father
James Prendergast

---

41. The word has been crossed out and is not legible.

24. From James Prendergast to his children in Boston

Mr Cornelius Riordan
N° 2 Shortstreet Boston
Massachusetts
N. America

Paid

Milltown 26th August 1845

My dear Children
On the 19th Instant I received your Letter of the 31st
of July with an enclosure of £5. We are all well thank
God and ˄I hope˄ this will find you all in good health. Your
Mother and I never forget in our prayers night and
day to beg of the Almighty to continue his favours to all
of you and to grant ye his blessing and protection. I
did not go to Killarney since I received your Letter,
but I suppose Riordan will not go out until the
beginning of next season and I will have the
blackthorn stick[42] for him to carry out to Thomas.
I would have gone to killarney since the arrival of
your Letter but I feared your Brother Mich^l would
suspect that I received a Letter. I did not let him
know any thing about it as I know he could
not be persuaded that I would not be the cause
of your not sending him some relief. He is
impatiently expecting an answer to my last letter.
He knows nothing about this and certainly I would
not write for some time but I judged that you would

---

42. Shillelagh.

wish to hear from us and to know whether
the check arrived with us. Your friends and
neighbours are all well and express their pleasure
at all times to hear that ye are all well.
My dear Children, your Mother joins with
me to send you our love and blessing and
I remain your
affectionate Father
James Prendergast

But within the last few weeks the greatest alarm
prevails throughout the kingdom.

JAMES PRENDERGAST,
October, 1845

25. From James Prendergast to his children in Boston

Mr Isaac Foster Stable Keeper
Devonshire street
(For Thomas Prendergast)
Boston
N. America

Paid

Milltown [. . .]^43

My dear Children
The receipt of your letter of 30th of September last [. . .]^44 highest ~~plea~~
pleasure, as nothing could give us greater comfort than to hear from ye as
often as possible, but we know your time is precious and that ye cannot
     write
as frequently as ye could^45 ∧wish∧. One thing in your Letter gave us
     considerable
trouble. It says that ye have but poor health. That troubled us
much, very much. If ye were less dutiful and less kind to [. . .]^46
ye are the feelings of parents would cause us to grieve for your
trouble. But when ye are what I may say without flattery, dutiful
tenderhearted and affectionate, our only support and the prop of our
old age, how alarmed must we feel for your safety when ye say
ye are not well. If your state of health be bad or continue so as not to
change for the better, We would advise ye to change your place and
come home. Nothing is so precious as health and without it the wealth
of the world can scarcely yield any comfort. We would prefer seeing
yourselves in good health to any interest or profit we could receive

---

43. The paper is torn. The letter's date is missing, but it is postmarked October 25, 1845, Tralee.
44. The paper is torn.
45. The word *could* is written over the word *would.*
46. The paper is torn.

while ye were in any danger. Your Mother and I pray daily
for the[47] preservation of your Health. May God grant our humble
request, and we hope that your own good sense will direct ye
how to act should health not grow better with ye. Your
Mother and I are well thank God and so are all your friends too
many to be named in particular. Maurice and his family are well
and still in the same situation. Your Brothers Michael is well if he
[. . .][48] is not ~~is not~~ the best but we must only
[. . .] family is well. As far as I could learn Margaret Forhan
[. . .] truth when she said she wrote home. Neither she
[. . .] Brothers sent a single penny tho' their mother
really wants it. The beginning of this Harverst was very promi[. . .].
The crops in general had a very rich appearance, and it was
generally expected that next season would be very plentiful.
But within the last few weeks the greatest alarm prevails
throughout the kingdom. It is dreaded that nothing less than
a famine must prevail next summer unless the Almighty
lord interpose. A disease has seized the potatoe crop which
was the standing food of the Country. The Potatoes which were good
and healthy a few days since are now rotten in the Ground. Even
some which were dug in beautiful dry weather and stored in Pits
seem to be affected with the same blight. The news papers teem
with alarming accounts of the same disease throughout the
kingdom. I cannot say whether the loss is equal to the alarm.
But dread of the greatest nature pervades all classes insomuch
that Parliament has been called upon to assemble to devise means
for providing against the dreaded calamity. May God in his mercy
avert such distress from his suffering poor. Dan Riordan is well
and so is Mr Spring and family. Every Letter which his children send
here contains accounts ˄of˄ every one of ye. We had an account here
a few days since, in a letter from Pat^k Quirk, that shortly

---

47. The word *the* is written over the word *your*.
48. The paper is torn.

[. . .]⁴⁹
[. . .] think it [. . .]
[. . .] believe it [. . .]
[. . .] next to hear whether she told truth [. . .]
statement. Philip Kelly begged if any of his [. . .]
ye would tell them that he is much troubled [. . .]
writes to him. I will not trouble ye further than to say [. . .]
your Mother joins with me in sending ye our blessing [. . .]
forgetting Julia and her Husband. I remain your
Affectionate Father
James Prenderg[. . .]⁵⁰

26. From James Prendergast to his children in Boston

Mʳ Cornelius Reardon
N° 16 Pearl Place Boston
Massachusetts
N. America

Paid

Milltown 27ᵗʰ Decʳ. 1845

My dear Children
Your letter of the 30ᵗʰ Novʳ last with its enclo
=sure of £8 stg. arrived with us on the 18ᵗʰ of Decʳ
Instant and was cashed for me without delay on the 22ⁿᵈ.
I must say that it was very timely for the christmas
holidays. Yet I will ‚tell‚ you and I hope you will

---

49. Owing to the torn paper, approximately five complete lines are missing, along with portions of the
    remaining lines on this page.
50. The paper is damaged where the letter was sealed.

believe me that we enjoyed greater pleasure than
the amount of the check could give when we read that
ye enjoyed good health. May the merciful Redeemer
preserve ye and shower his favours on ye. Considering
our age your Mother ₍and I₎ are well thank God. Your Brothers
and their families are so likewise, and so is Dan Riordan.
He is always at M͏ʳ Finns. M͏ʳ Spring and family are
very well. Your Aunt is still in Cork. I have only heard
from her she received some sort of a hurt. I hear she is lame
but I could not learn how it happened. As for the
state of the country it is very uncertain. In harvest
the crops were so promising that people thought the ensuing
year would be plentiful and cheap. But before Sep͏ʳ It was
discovered that the potatoe crop was rotting in the ground.
The complaint became general throughout Ireland and
not without cause. The public papers teem with acc͏ᵗˢ
of the loss in various parts of this kingdom. Government sent
out Commissioners to try to discover the cause and means
to prevent it but all in vain. A dread of famine pre
=vailed throughought kingdom. Petitions crowded in from
all parts of the kingdom, Praying that Government would
open the Ports and grant a free Trade. The Cabinet council
disagreed and resigned their places. A new Cabinet was
attempted to ₍be₎ formed, but it said that the attempt failed
and the old council was recalled. Great confusion prevails
here as nothing certain is yet done. No scarcity appears
in our part of the country yet thank God. But the spring
and summer it is dreaded will be very dear as great
quantities of Potatoes have been lost in every part
of the count[r]y. It was not a partial complaint
but a general one and I am really sorry to say
it is not without cause. I will not trouble you
with further accounts only that your Mother and I daily
offer our prayers for your preservation and now join

in sending you our love and blessing. I remain
my dear children
yours truly and affectionately
James Prendergast

27. From James Prendergast to his children in Boston

Mr Cor^s Riordan
N° 16 Pearlplace
Boston Massachusetts
N. America

Paid

Milltown 11th August 1846

My dear Children
I received your Letter of the 16th of July on the 2nd of this
Month. I presented the check at the National Bank Tralee last
week. The Manager Mr Quill said that it was payable in Cork
However he paid me the compliment of advancing me the amount
as he usually does and transmitted the check on his own acc^t
to Cork. He charged me nothing for his trouble. He refused even
the postage of the Letter which I offered to pay. My dear Children
nothing can give ˄us˄ greater pleasure than to hear that ye are well
and enjoying good health. May God continue his favours to
you all. My dear Children your Mother and I are in
much better health now than ˄when˄ we wrote last. I may say,
thank God, that we are now perfectly recovered from our illness.
Your Brothers and their respective families are well
and so are all your friends. Your Cousin Francis Hurly
(Jerry's son) is to take holy orders this week. On Saturday next
he comes to the Altar (for the first time) a priest. Sometime

since he intended going to america and received an Exeat[51]
for a foreign mission. But since that time he was
countermanded and is now kept on the home mission
to the great joy of his parents and friends. He is a very
fine man and it is expected will be a good priest.
The state of the Country is not as distressing as was dreaded
in the beginning of this year, but that was owing to the
supplies[52] of foreign provisions brought into the Country
and to the public works carried on to give the poor em
=ployment. Relief committees were formed in every locality
and the Board of Works empowered them to repair byroads
and carry on different other works of public utility, to
employ the labouring classes young and old, and to give
them food for their labour. These arrangements were well
observed, and real distress was scarcely known here, thank
God. Even the markets were kept down to reasonable
prices for such as did not labour. But unless some
such measures be taken to provide against next years greater
fears are entertained for the coming than the present season.
The Potatoe crop is much worse than the last. The disease that
was not perceived until September, and even December in other
places last year is now complained of throughout the Country.
It is felt more severely as we have not the fourth part of
last years produc even diseased. We expect good measures from
the British parliament this year but we mus wait to know
the issue. Our Irish members stood their post well and
were not unsuccessful. My dear Children I will say no more
than that your Mother joins with me to send you our blessing
and so do your Brothers and that I remain affectionately
your Father
James Prendergast

---

51. Exeat: a letter of permission allowing a cleric to transfer from one diocese to another.
52. The word *supplies* is written over another word, probably *foreign*.

28. From James Prendergast to his children in Boston

Mr Cornelius Riordan N° 16
Pearlplace Boston
State of Massachusetts
N. America

prepaid

Milltown 20th Novr 1846

My dear Children
On the 11th of August last I wrote in reply
to your letter of the 16th of July, thanking you
for your Remittance which was ~~a relief~~
a relief received most timely. Since that time
We were most anxiously expecting an answer
from ye. At last our patience was worn out
and we became really alarmed, not for any
disappointment of our own, but lest any
disaster should befal either of you and cause
this unusual delay. We are now old and must
of course be near our dissolution and we
would descend quietly to the grave if we knew
that ye were well. John Payne arrived here
some time since. He said ye were well, and
that he heard Tom was married, but could
not say it absolutely. Therefore my dear Children
We entreat you to write on receipt of this and ease our
troubled minds. Say if either of the boys married. If
so may God bless them. The state of this Country
is almost beyond description. Nothing to be seen in
all quarters but distress and destitution. Famine and

starvation threatening everywhere unless God mercifully
send some foreign aid. Last year was a year of
abundance and plenty when compared with the present.
This year all the potatoe crop was lost. The best farmer
here is as short of them as the poorer class. Potatoes
are seldom in market and ˄the few˄ that then come are bought
by the rich as a rarity at the rate of from 8^d to 12^d p^r stone
Flour rates at 3/3^s p^r stone and varies from that to 2/8^s for
flour not much superior to bran. Oatmeal 3/3^s and all
other foods dear accordingly. The supply of the country
it is dreaded will soon be exhausted unless supplies
are brought in from abroad. The grain crop of
this country fell very short this year. The
last remittance ye sent is out long since and we are
considerably in debt. Therefore if ye can assist us
as usual do not delay your usual relief.
The Pawn offices here are so stocked with Goods that
10^s could scarcely be raised on the value of five Pounds.
Let Con know that his Brother is well and in his usual
place. All the friends are well. It be too numerous
to name them particularly. Your Cousin Jerry Hurlys
son received orders of priesthood in September last.
He is now Father Francis and stationed at Cahir
=siveen. My dear Children your Mother joins
me to send ye all our blessing as well as
if we named ye severally not forgetting
Con, and I remain affectionately
your father
James Prendergast

29. From James Prendergast to his children in Boston

Mr Cornelius Rirodan 16 Pearlplace
Boston
State of Massachusetts
N. America

Paid

Milltown 21st April 1847

My dear Children
With perfect gratitude and paternal affection I acknowledge
the receipt of your favour of the 30th of March last. I must
say that your filial care has placed your aged parents beyond
the reach of distress for the ensuing summer notwithstanding
the extreme dearness of every article of food. It is needless to
say any thing about the markets. They are nearly the same as
heretofore, however any change that is seems to be for the better
[. . .]⁵³ distress prevails here in consequence of disease
[. . .]reasing in this locality, insomuch that
[. . .] people are falling without dis[. . .]⁵⁴
[. . .]poor, fever and dysentery are
[. . .]our and it is thought that a
[. . .] throughout this country the
[. . .]a that a person formerly
[. . .]form. But blessed
[. . .] reason to be thank
[. . .] that she was

---

53. The letter is torn. A large portion is missing.
54. The word is illegible. It may have been crossed out.

[. . .]is evening. It is the
first time for the last nine weeks. I hope she will get on rapidly.
I would have written before I received yours but waiting to
be able to send an account how her illness would terminate.
Your Brother Mich[l] left this place easter monday to sail for
America. He thought to stop until he could have certain account
to carry, but we pressed him to go, as we knew that if he
remained, what he had would be spent and he should
remain the rest of his days ˄in misery.˄ I gave her the ten shillings [. . .] [55]
ordered for Mich[l] ˄to his Wife,˄ and to do her justice, she was as
attentive to your Mother during her illness as any daugh
=ter could be. Maurice and his family are well. He is
daily getting better. I gave him the three Pounds. It was a
relief he did not expect. It raised ˄him˄ fr[. . .] [56] if
blessings be of any value his [. . .]
them forth for ye hourly [. . .]
I are thankful. We co[. . .]
ye all, for the ampl[. . .]
I am sure we[57] can [. . .]
now as well [. . .]
Joanna Hurly [. . .]
a noble ch[. . .]
us. Give [. . .]
children. In your next let us know if Mich[l] reached Boston
and how he fared during his passage. I need say nothing to
you about John's death. Mich[l] can tell you every thing.
I went to his Wife and asked if she would suffer her
child to go to America. She said she would let her come

---

55. The word is illegible. It may have been crossed out.
56. The letter is torn. A large portion is missing.
57. The word *we* is written over the word *I*.

to myself but would be unfond to let her go to America, however
that she would consider for some. I released some frocks of hers that
were pawned and I intend bringing her. She is a fine child and
much like her father in her way. I must always have an eye to
her. She is the only one now living that was called after your
Mother Elizabeth. Let Mich¹ know that ~~Mich¹~~ his Wife and
Children all well. Write to us at all times and tell
[. . .]⁵⁸ how ye are. Your letters without are welcome [. . .]⁵⁹
[. . .]aden. To hear from ye is our life and joy.
[. . .]ith me to ₐgiveₐ ye all our love and
[. . .] affectionately
your father
[. . .]es Prendergast

30. To Michael Prendergast—probably written by his brother Thomas

Boston June ₐtheₐ 14 – 47

My Dear Brother Michael
I Read your letter of the 7 in^st on this morning.
I need not tell you we were glad that you
arrived safe. Dear Michael we send you inclos[. . .]⁶⁰
in this letter too 5 Doller bills of the Bank of
St. Stephens⁶¹ and you are better have it shan
-ged. Mr Warlock will Have the goodness to Direct

---

58. The letter is torn. A large portion is missing.
59. The paper is damaged where the letter was sealed.
60. The paper is damaged and the end of the word is missing.
61. Paper currency issued by a private bank.

you and loose no time in coming to Boston.
Dear Michael ˄it˄ is all we could spare after send
-ing Home to my Father. Tell C Mahony that we
could not do any thing for him. If we could we
would. Tell Mr [. . .] [62] that C. Reordon
would be oblight [. . .] have the
kindness to Dire[. . .] and
Quickest to Bost[. . .]
I Rem[. . .]

62. This fragment of a letter is torn. Portions of the four
last lines are missing, as well as the signature and the
address.

LETTER 30. Written to Michael in St. John, New Brunswick. It was sent by his brothers and was probably written by Thomas. It is the only letter from Boston in the collection.

Boston June 14 - 43

My Dear Brother Micheal

I Read your letter of the 7 inst on this morning
need not tell you we were glad that you
rived Safe Dear Micheal we send you inclos
this letter too 5 Dollers bills of the Bank of
t. Stephens and you are better have it than
d Mr Warlock will have the goodness to Direct
and loose no time in Coming to Boston
Dear Micheal it is all we could spare after send
Home to My Father tell L Mahony that we
uld not do any thing for him if we could we
ould tell Mr   that L Reordon
uld be oblighd   have the
dness to Direct   and
ciest to Bros
J Rei

31. From James Prendergast to his children in Boston

Mr Cornelius Riordan 16
Pearlplace Boston
State of Massachusetts
N. America

Paid

I forgot to mention
that I got the white
flannell petticote[63]

Milltown 25th July 1847

My dear Children
I now write you that I may enjoy the pleasure of hearing by your
reply that ye are well for really I think it an age since I received
the last communication. Also your Mother and I feel very uneasy
on account of your Brother Mich^l. About the 27th of March
last he left home and delayed a few days only in Cork before He sailed
for St John's New Brunswick, as we heard. Since that time we never
heard from him. We expected an account long since either by
Letter from himself or thro ye, but we were really disappointed. We
are really alarmed on his account. He left 4 children and their
poor Mother, with no more subsistence than nine shillings. This was
a very poor stock, even[64] if the year were much more plentiful.
We could not see them suffering without feeling for their
wants. But our hope is in God. We expect better news
at least when ye reply to this if we hear not sooner.

---

63. These three lines—a postscript—appear on the address leaf, on what would have been the back of
    the folded letter.
64. The word *even* is written over the word *if.*

Your Mother and I are now perfectly recovered from the severe
and lingering illness under which we laboured, and thank God,
we are in as good health as could be expected, at the present
period of our lives. Ye will add to our comfort by answering this
as speedily as ye can, and sending whatever account ye can
of Mich$^{l's}$ state. Maurice and all his family were success
=sively lying in fever. They are now recovering thank
God and I hope out of danger tho Maurice himself is still
languid and complaining of pains in all his Bones after his fit.
They may thank ye for their lives as the part they received
of what ye sent was a principal means to recover them.
The markets here are still rather high, tho a reduction has taken
place here. We cannot say much of the present crops of
the country. They were very promising until within the few last
days when some signs of a blight appeared on the potatoe stalks
not very unlike that which destroyed them last year. It is
too soon to know how it may terminate, however we must
trust in God and hope for the best. Dan Riordan is
well and still in the same situation. Last wednesday the
trunk which Julia sent arrived here. It was carried to
Waterford by the captain who refused to give it up in Tralee
saying it was entered for that custom house. Mr Riordan
had a good deal of trouble to bring it up here. It cost us
every way £1..5^s. Mr Riordan desired to let Julia know that
the captain charged freight tho Mr Riordan said he was sure
that he was paid a greater compliment by ye than what would
discharge the freight. The Trunk contained as follows viz Three
Gowns and a quilled black silk petticoat two shawls, two handsome
hand kerchiefs, two bedgowns four shifts, two shirts three waist
=coats a black silk hand kerchief, a fine sheet 2 pair shoes
a pair of black woven stockings a cap a trashbag and black ribbon
and an Apron. From the appearance of the trunk I really believe it
was not stirred. Her Mother says ˌsheˌ feels as ˌifˌ she were only 20 years

when she wears on part of what she knows to have belonged
to her child. She desires to return Julia her grateful thanks
for her precious Gifts and I am sure I have a right to do the
same for her present to me. She joins with me to send all and
every one of our children our love and blessing, and not
forgetting Con and Tom's Wife whom we deem our children
also. May the merciful God bless, protect and preserve ye
is the constant prayer we offer.
I remain my dear Children, affectionately
your father
James Prendergast
P.S. I expect a speedy reply and desire ye will
try and discover Mich[l] if he has not arrived with
ye before th[. . .][65]

32. From James Prendergast to his children in Boston

M[r] Cornelius Riordan N° 16
Boston
Pearlplace State of Massachusetts
N. America

Paid

Milltown 21st August 1847

My dear Children
Your Mother and myself never enjoyed greater pleasure than ˄when˄ we
    heard from
ye, and I must confess that never a letter gave us greater comfort than your

---

65. The paper is damaged where the letter was originally folded.

last one dated 30th July. From the acc^{ts} daily arriving here of the great
mortality prevailing in America we gave up Michael as lost, but thank the
great God we are now easy as we are sure He is well and with ye. We
have other causes of pleasure also, you have a young son, may God spare
    him
as a Comfort to his parents, and the parents to nurture him, and tho his
    Grandmother
and I cannot have the pleasure of seeing him and giving him our blessing,
    I assure you
that both of us pray for him and send him our blessing. You also say that
    Jeffry is
married. That gives us additional pleasure, moreover as we fondly hope
    that He
has married with the advice of the rest, and as you give us such a good
    character
of his wife. The name of Conway was always most respectable in this
    county,
and next to Kerry, Tipperary is the only county in Ireland I love best. The
Inhabitants of Kerry and Tipperary are always the same as Brothers. Give
    them
both our blessing. Hitherto I have not spoken of Con or Julia, the subject
    did not allow
me untill now, but believe me I have them as much at heart ~~as much~~ as any
of my⁶⁶ children. I can never forget ye as long as I live. Your Mother and
I pray for ye daily. You seem to doubt that your Mother lives. She does
thank God. I would be poorly if she did not. I would not deny it on
any acc^t. She was very sick for about 3 Months. No great hopes were
entertained of her recovery, but thank God she is well now. She
was only recovering slowly when I was laid sick and I was somewhat
delirious for 11 Weeks, however I recovered thank God. We wanted
nothing. Ye sent us the means and we wanted it. Maurice and his

---

66. The word *my* is written over the word *them*.

family live still in the same place but they have no employ
=ment. John Lynch has nothing to do. Maurice and his family
were successively lying in fever, each of ˏthemˏ got a relapse
two or three times. Your Mother sent out Nell West, nursetender,
to attend Maurice who was the first that got sick. She remained
there until the last was well. They can never return ye
thanks. It was ˏwhatˏ ye sent your Mother and me that kept
them alive. We had ˏto lookˏ to the old and young. We could not see
them in want without sharing with them while we had it.
That leaves us pennyless. What ye sent us is nearly gone.
John's Wife and child are well. They live in Tralee. Michael's
Family are well. I could not describe the feelings of his Wife and
children on hearing that he was well. His fatherinlaw was
complaining of illness for some days before the letter arrived
but on hearing from him the poor man seemed to get fresh life
and never since complained of disease. His Motherinlaw is
as well as he left her. The kitchen gardens were tilled and grew
but they were damaged like last year. They are dug up now and
if we had more we cannot say much about the crops yet.
They grow up, but as only small quantities of Potatoes were
sown last season none of them is coming into our market yet. The
accounts about them are various. The Trunk which Julia sent
arrived here some time ago after a deal of trouble. I stated every
thing about it in a letter which I sent off in July, and which I
am sure you received about the first of this Month. Tell
Con that Dan Riordan is well and still in the same place.
Maurice Mahony boot and shoemaker, and his cousin, Sons to Daniel
and James Mahony of Rathpogue sailed for Boston in May
last. They never sent any account home. I would be glad if
to hear in your next if you should meet either of them. Their fa
=milies are good neighbours. I am very sorry to hear that young Pat^k
Heffernan of Rathpogue died within a few hours sail of Quebec

and my poor friend Mary Connor, Sister to Jerry Connor late of
Milltown who was going to her Brothers to Hamilton, I heard
died after landing. The accounts of deaths daily received here are
really terrifying. Write to us without delay. We will be very
uneasy until we hear from ye again and let us know whether
Mich^l got any return of his illness. Your Mother joins with
me in sending ye our love and blessing and desiring to be kindly
remembered to each of our Children, Con, Julia, Mich^l, Jeffry and ye, and
not forgetting those members whom we never yet saw, Jeffry's Wife,
yours, and her babe, young James. May God bless and preserve
ye all. I remain my dear Children
affectionately
your Father
James Prendergast
Thos Prendergast
Boston &c.
P.S. Mich^l's Wife and family ˄desire˄ that he will soon write to
let them know how he is.

. . . she and children would lose the little relief
allowed them by the course of the Law.

JAMES PRENDERGAST,
September, 1847

33. From James Prendergast to his children in Boston

Mr Cornelius Riordan
16 Pearlplace Boston
State of Massachusetts
N. America

prepaid

Milltown 26th Sepr 1847

My dear Children
I received your Letter of the 31st August last with a check
for £10 which Cor^s Murphy took up and sent to Liverpool and
we had ˄to˄ allow 3/4^s that is 4^d to the Pound, so that we received
£9..16^s..8^d and Maurice received his part as soon as the return
arrived. He returns ye his thanks and blessing and so he ought,
for it was what ye sent kept him and family alive. At all times
I shared with him. He is in raptures for saying ye sent for his
son James, and the Boy himself is most anxious for the
call. He will be ready as soon as ye send and I hope
he will shew himself worthy of being called out. He is
active, strong, and I think both graceful and grateful.
I need not say that your Mother and I can enjoy no pleasure
equal to that of hearing from ye at all times. We should be
the last of parents if we did not allow what every one
here does that ye are the best children that left this
country for the last 100 years. Those who never saw ye
or knew ye, are thankful to ye and pray for ye in consequence
of the kindness ye have shewn us. Michael's family are all
well. His fatherinlaw and motherinlaw are as attentive to the
children as if they were their own and between them and us
they feel no want as yet. His Wife is well and she says she is content

as He arrived safe, and that she is sure of his assistance as soon as
he can [67] send it.

I understand that the Rev[d] Bartholomew OConnor our
p.p. is going out to America in the course of a few days, on a
mission from his Bishop and therefore if Mich[l] will
write to his ˄wife˄ his best way will be to address it to me to be
forwarded to his Wife. If he addressed to any other person
in Town, they are all members of Committee, and if his
letter contained any thing she and children would lose the
little relief allowed them by the course of the Law. A letter
addressed to herself would reach her as well as
if addressed to any other. If the Priest M[r] OConnor
should visit ye, ye need not lose much to him
on our account. We were under no compliment to him.
Remember us to every one of the family. Do not forget our
late daughters, tho we never had the pleasure of seeing them.
I mean Tom and Jeffry's Wives. They are two names, Cotter
and Conwey already connected with our family, and
respected in this place. I have not spoken of Con or
Julia, for if they be last in my words, they are not in
my affection. May God bless the entire of my chil
=dren, and their offspring. When ye write next let us know
how my child young James (Tom) is. I hope Mich[l] will
write to his Wife as soon as he can. A letter arrived
here stating that Edm[d] Moriarty Brother to John Murphy
of Ballyverane was in a very bad state of health.
He is the son of respectable Parents and a near
Relative of your own (his mother was a Thompson and
Grandmother Spring). I would be glad that ye should enquire
and let us know whether he is dead or alive. Ye will get

---

67. The word *can* is written over the word *could*.

every information from Maurice OBrien Soninlaw to Farrel
McHugh of Drominbeg. If [68] ye know not OBrien ye can hear where
be is by applying to Dan¹ Buckly N° 3 Breadstreet. If
ye can get any account of Edm^d Moriarty send it in your
next. I need not say any thing about the state of the
country as I have nothing to add to what I stated
in my last letter which I suppose arrived with ye
about the time that I received yours. McHugh wrote
to his children a few days since. Your Mother joins
me in sending ye our blessing and I remain
affectionately
your father
James Prendergast

34. From James Prendergast to his children in Boston, and from Ellen Prendergast to her husband Michael

Mr Cornelious Riordn
N° 16 Pearl Place
America   Boston Mass

Paid

Milltown Bleach Road [69]

My D^r children I received your letter of the
30th November 47 and am happy to hear you are all
well as this leaves me and your mother Thanks be to

---

68. The word *If* is written over the word *ye*.
69. This letter (really two letters in one) is not dated, but is postmarked Tralee, December 29, 1847.

God. I receive £7..o..o four pounds for me self two
pounds for Michales wife and one pound for
Maurice which I have Delivered According to your
Directions. Not forgeting young James you sent no
Acc^t of him in this letter nor any Acc^t of your wifes
which ~~which~~ which would give year mother and
me the greatest pleasure of hearing from you all
and to have all the names mentioned when
you writing. Alls I wish verry much to have a letter
from Con and Julia. I need not say any thing about
Maurice in this letter as he is to write to ye himself
but surley him and family was in their Grave only
for the Assistance he rec^d from ya. Now my D^r
children I am your Fathe I send you all my Blessing.
Your mother also sends you all her Blessing and joins
me in love to you all and I can Assure you we had not
one shilling to spare when we rec^d this last welcome
letter. I wis to have an Answer to this letter as soon as
Possible and let me know how is Mich^{ls} Health in that
country. So my D^r children ˅I remain˅ your loveing Father
James Prendergast

Milltown Bleach Road

My Dr Mich^l It gave me great Pleasure
to hear from you. I rec^d two pound from your father
which was verry much wanting to me and the
children. Me self nor the children got none of the
relief male[70] these four months past. The comitee

---

70. Meal: Ellen is referring to imported cornmeal that was distributed under the authority of a locally
    based famine relief committee.

for givun relief came to a plan and kept male
from the famileys of Every man that went to
America. My father and mother are in verry bad
Health. Me father is not able to work these six
months past. I could not stand a tall were it not
for the Assistance I got from my Peopleinlaw and
from my Father. Now the times are so bad I cant
Expect any more from them so I Expect yowill
write as soon as possible for the children ˄are˄ Bare and
Naked from cloaths and when you are writing
Direct your letter to me self. The three young
children are after a long sickness and are now
recovered. So my Dr Husband I conclude by reman
your love wife Ellen Prendergast
N.B John James Hurly of Killorglan
is Dead Burried on this Day month

Milltown Bleach Road

My Dr Mich[l] It gave Me great Pleasu[re]
to hear from you I Rec[eive]d two pound from your [which]
which was verry Much wanting to me and [to]
Children Me Self Nor the Children got None of
Relief Male these four Months past the Commi[ttee]
for Gevem Relief Came to a plan and Kept W[omen]
from the familys of Every Man that went [to]
America My father and Mother are in Verry [bad]
Health Me father is Not able to Work these 5
Months past I could Not Stand a tall were it
for the Assistance I got from My People and [?]
from My Father Now the times are So bad I ca[nt]
Expect any More from thene So I Expect you w[ill]
write as Soon as possible for the Children are Bare
Naked from Cloaths and when you are Wri[ting]
Direct your letter to Me Self the thru y[our]
Children are after a long Sickness and are No[t]
Recovered, So My Dr Husband I Conclude by [?]
Your love wife Ellen Prendergast

N. B John James Hurly of Killorglen
is Dead Burried on this Day Month

LETTER 34. Sent to Boston by James Prendergast and Ellen Prendergast (Michael's wife). It differs from the majority of the letters in that it was not written by one of the known scriveners. Its language is less formal than that in the letters dictated to Connell or Mahoney.

Mr Cornelious Riordan
No 96 Pearl Place
America   Boston Mass

Milltown Bleach Road

My Dr Children I received your letter of the
9th November 47 and am happy to hear you are all
well as this leaves Me and your Mother Thanks be to
God, I Received £4=0=0 four pounds for Me Self two
pounds for Michales Wife and One pound for
Maurice which I have Delivered According to your
Directions. Not forgeting young James you sent No
Acct of him in this letter nor any Acct of your wifes
which which which would give Year Mother and
Me the Greatest pleasure of hearing from you all
and to have all the Names Mentioned when
you writing also I wish verry Much to have a letter
from Con and Julia I nued Not Say any thing about
Maurice in this letter as he is to write to Yee himself
but Surley him and family was in their Grave only
for the Asistance he Rec from Yee, Now My Dr
Children I am your Fathe I Send You all My Blessing
your Mother also Sends you all her Blessing and Joins
Me in love to you all And I Can Assure you we had not
one Shilling to Spare when we Rec This last welcome
letter I wis to have an Answer to this letter as Soon as
Possible and lete Me Know how is Michls Health in that
Country Sorry Dr Children your loveing Father
                        James Prendergast

35. From Maurice Prendergast to his siblings in Boston

Mr Cornelius Riordan
N° 16 Pearl Place
Boston State of
Massachusetts
N^o America

Paid
prepaid

Dromin December 26th 1847

My Dear brothers an sister I take the opportunity
of writing you these few lines hoping to find
you all and yours in as good health as this
at present leavs me and family Father an
Mother an my Brother Michaels family. My
Dear brothers I nead not say any more about
them as I know he is going to write himself on this
Day. My Dear Con I was at no loss in finding it to
be my Duty to return you thanks for what
you have Done for me that I can never forget
but I left it to my father as he told me he would
have done so. This is large an great kind and affecti
onate moreso than I can mention at present. My
Dear Con the last Three pounds was a total
means of recovering me an my family. I assure
you it gave my poor Father a chearful counten
ance when handing it over to me. I might commin˄ce˄
with ~~year~~ ˄year˄ joint kindness before an after. My
Dear brothers I should have sold my cow on the
26th of April last. Fortunate to me that ye were

the purchaser before the sale Day came an tha‸t‸
left me an my family not want for Drink
when the Day came round that Mrs Lynch
was kind enough to milk her an send it to the
Door to us. I dare say you are aware from the
export from that country you are in what Irela‸nd‸
must be. These times would become a green colour
to me were it not for year kindness
to me. It have been more like children
than brothers or sister. My Dear Thomas I would
be curius to let me know how Con and Judy look
in personal appearance whether the change of
Climate has made any change in them for better
or worce also Jeffery and you. Also let me know
how Michaels health is. It was not a bit to
good before he left. You will not have any
objection in leting us know if your son James
is a stout fellow as I should hope he is an who
he is like. I should hope for Jefferys addition to
the family at the answering of this or thereabo‸ut.‸
The reason I ask those silly Favours of you as
I suppose you will be set to work when
answering this as being the minor as Poor
John youst call you. I asure you I dont
forget him. The thought of him often givs
me a lonely feel. I hope you all pray for
him. My Dear brothers ‸and sister‸ you cannot think
how strong my Father an Mother are after
the long fight the made an the heavy fit
of illness. The may thank god an ye for
that recovery. Ye talked of taking James
out but it is so hard for me to expected
it from all you have done for me up to

this Day. I might say that ye have been my
chief support for the last nine months. I
asure ye their is not a time we bend a knee
but [we] [71] pray for ye. I hope the lord will
hear us an grant. Should any plan be adopte‸d‸
it would be a matter of great importance
to me to take James out as I see no prospec‸t‸
of his being able to do any good here. I am not
employed mself since the begining of my
Illness that comminced with me about
the 15th of January last though I am in as
perfect health an as active as ever I was than‸ks‸
be to god. I nead not tell you were the time‸s‸
better that I would not walk about ~~were~~
~~the times better~~ though I had spent seven
months on the flat of my back. Should
James get out it might be means of geting
myself out later or earlier. Daniel Riordan
is in good health. You cannot think how we‸ll‸
he looks. I forgot to tell you that Jeffery
was the only person that escaped Faver.
Every individual in the house were Down together
but him. I hope you will write me a long letter.
Direct it to my Father. I will say no more at
present. My family joins me to send you all our
blessings. Remember me to the entire Family.
I remain your affectionate
Brother Maurice Prendergast [72]

---

71. As written, the word is *ye*.
72. The closing salutation and signature are written sideways over the text on the third page of the letter.

36. From Ellen Prendergast to her husband Michael, and from James Prendergast to his children in Boston

Mr Thomas Prendergast
16 Pearlplace Boston
State of Massachusetts
N. America

prepaid
Paid

Milltown 4th Feby 1848

My Dear Husband
On Wednesday last I received your Letter of the
11th February last with its enclosed order of £13.
Of that sum I got £8 and the rest was disposed
of as directed. The children and I were really distressed
and would be very poorly situated had not your father
and Mother taken care of us. They never left us depending
on any friend without sharing with us. I must only
say that between them and my Father and Mother The
children and I were better situated than many that
boasted of Independance. My dear Husband, It is true
that the relief ye sent was timely yet believe
me it was not half so welcome ˄as the acc^t˄ that ye were all
well. Your Parents, Mine, The Children, myself,
your Brother Maurice and Family are well. Johnny
is what you never expected to see him, now the very
best you left. He is able to be with your Father every
moment and cares for nobody but, as he says, for his
grandfather and Grandmother. My dear Husband, you

desire me make what I could out of what you sent
but it is really impossible to do any thing now
in this place. Everything requires a good capital
in this season of the year, but as soon as the
season comes on I will do as much as I can. Write
very often. We will be better pleased to hear that ye
all are well than any gift without that acc^t. Julia
is very well attends the Convent school regularly and is
considered to be daily improving. I will say no more than that
I send you your Brothers and their Wives and my sister Julia
and Con (not the last in my affections) my blessing
and that I am affectionately and obediently
your wife
Ellen Prendergast
P.S. Julia says she hopes that she will never die
but with aunt Julia.

My dear Children
You can perceive by the first part of this letter ~~from~~
(to your Brother Mich^l from his Wife) that your letter
arrived and that its contents was disposed of as ye
directected. She stated truth in what she said. We are all well
thank God, and I need not say that we can never have pleasure
equal to that of hearing that ye are well. Father B. OConnor sent
four Letters since he went to Boston. One to the Convent one to
Father Buckley, one to Mrs Moriarty, and the 4th to his nephew
OConnor of Aglish. In each he said that ye are a credit to
the Land of your birth, that ye received him, after his fatigue
and hardships, as kindly as if ye were more than his cousins.
I am glad ye did so for it was not an act lost. For that rea
son I will be glad that ye will, in future, shew him the
respect due from parishioners. Tell him that the Ladies of

the Convent, Father Buckley, Mrs Moriarty and family and
his nephew with the rest of his friends are well and that
his parishioners, the most respectable, as well as the most
humble, pray daily for his safe return. Dan Riordan is well.
We have acc^{ts} from him always thro Maurice. Your Mother and I are
much stronger than you could expect us to to be. She says she
would be ten years younger if she could once hold young James
and that she is really thankful to father Batt for saying he was
a real true blue, or Old James. Maurice desires to return ye
sincere thanks from himself and family as it was your Bounty
preserved them in their last illness when distress was
so general. His son James is in raptures expecting th[. . .]⁷³
ye will send for him. So are his parents. Your Mother
joins me in desiring to desiring to be remembered to each of our
daughters inlaw and in sending our love and blessing to them and
ye and not forgetting Con and Julia from we wish to hear
as often as they or ye can send us an account. My dear
Children I will conclude by saying that
I am affectionately
your Father
James Predergast
James Prendergast⁷⁴

---

73. The paper is damaged where the letter was sealed.
74. The letter is signed twice.

37. From James Prendergast to his children in Boston

Mr Thomas Prendergast
N° 16 Pearlplace
Boston
State of Massachusetts
N. America

prepaid
T.S.P.

Milltown 18th June 1848

My dear Children
I receiv^d your letter of the 30th of May last containing a check
for seven Pounds. It was a timely relief and tho I wanted
it I assure ˌyouˌ I felt more on your account than I did on my
own account. I feared that some mishap had befallen
ye as I heard not from ye for a long time. I was in debt
one pound nineteen shillings which I borrowed time
after time, since what you sent me was spent. I
was in a very bad state of health and I feared I would
have died before your relief would reach me and that
I would be a burthen on the parish for my funeral necessary
but, thank God, I [. . .]⁷⁵ received a new life when I
received your letter and not so much on account of
the order, as on account of the account it contains
that ye are all well. It is always said that he
who has ~~tenderful~~ and careful children is happy. In
that case I am really so, for my sons and daughter
are so and I will say that I have two of the

---

75. The word is crossed out.

best children in the world, while I have
Julia and Con. My dear children ye can be
neither jealous nor displeased when I say
that I am more thankful to him than to my[. . .]⁷⁶
own. At the same time I have cause to thank
you all. Mr Quill Manager of the National Bank
cashed the Bill for your Mother on yesterday. She
is so well that she left this place yesterday morning
and arrived here in the Evening with the amount of her
order. James Maurice was here. She gave ₐhim₎ the
three Pounds which ye ordered to carry to his father. Also
the letter which ye sent ₐ(to his father)₎ arrived here early in the evening
and he carried it. His father said before this that he
wrote to ye consenting and praying that ye would take
out the boy. James himself said so on yesterday. It
is the only wish of the Boy. Ye need ₐnot₎ delay to
send for him as ₐsoon₎ ye receive this for I assure ₐye₎ it is
the wish of all his family both father and Mother
as well as himself. His father will write
directly and I am sure ye will have his
letter, unless it miscarry, sooner than mine. If
he were over once He ought to help his own
family and free ye from a part of your cares
here on this side. He desires to remember him to his
aunt Julia and uncle Con and adds that every one
of his family have the same wish as, in gratitude
and every other respect as they are more indebted
to Con than to their own blood relatives for his kind
=ness. James says if he were with ye he would
try to shew ye that he knows what he and his
family owe ye for your kindness and good natures.

---

76. The letters are crossed out.

Mich^{ls} Wife and children are well, and so are his fatherinlaw
and Motherinlaw. They are really attentive to children. His Wife
is as attentive to us as our daughter could be. They
are doing well and would be glad to hear daily
if possible from him. Tell Mich^l that he ought
not forget Mich^l Ginnaw for 18 shillings which
was due to him when Mich^l left here. He knows
that I am bound for it and that only Mich^l Ginna
is so indulgent he should have been paid
long since, but he should not be forgotten
on that account. Your Mother and I may say,
every individual of our family both maurice
and Mich^{ls} join with me in sending a sincere
blessing to every one of their beloved family (the
young and old) praying that the eldest
members may live long and the youngest
to be as old. I will on say I am
Affectionately
your Father
James Prendergast

Yes and it would be a proud hour to him and to me,
to have him leave this poor and forlorn country.

Maurice Prendergast,
June, 1848

38. From Maurice Prendergast to his sister Julia's husband, Cornelius Riordan

To Mr Corn^s Riordan
Boston
To the care of Thos Prendergast
N° 16 Pearl place state mass
Boston

P.P.
Dromin June 22nd 1848

Killarney
Dromin June 22nd 1848

My Dear Brother~~-in-law~~ sisters Husband
I must say that I am proud of you, for I can
say that you always acted a good man since
the day you joined us. I return you my warmest thanks for the 3£ you now sent me thro
my Brother Thos. [...]⁷⁷ ₐnotₐ forgetting your many
kindnesses, I must say that only for it, I would
be very badly off. I am out of employment for
the last 18 months. I laboured out of that time for
8 months with ill health, but now I am quite
recovered and in as good health as ever, tho I can
inform you that our country is in a most deplorable
state with poverty and want of employment after
2 years Famine and pestilence stricken down, our poor
houses loaded or t[h]ronged, our gaols filled, people
only doing crime to get something to eat or to be

---

77. The word or words are crossed out.

transported prefering it to be a better life. Now
my Dear Con you will be good enough to return
my Brothers my sincere thanks for their help to
me. My Brother Tho⁵ mentioned to me about
sending
for my son James. Yes and it would be a proud
hour to him and to me, to have him leave this poor
and forlorn country. My Father and Mother is in perfect
health, but their doom would be in their grave
only for you, and family of friends and if they lived
the poor house would be their doom, where you
would see many a desent person well reared,
his food only indian corn porrage [78] and water with
a little treacle, with a felons jacket. Our country
is in a most poor state. Nothing grieves me now
so much but Mich conduct after the faithful
promise he made.
I remain your affectionate
Brother-in-law
Maurice Prendergast
P.S. Remember me to my Brothers and my one only
sister Julia and to their familys. My entire
family joins in their best love in this letter
to you beyond the seas and I expect a return
by post as soon as you can.
Direct my letter as usual
to my Father for me.

---

78. Promoted as a substitute food after the failure of the potato crop, it was made from imported corn meal.

39. From James Prendergast to his children in Boston

Mʳ Thomas Prendergast
Foster's Stables
Devonshire street
Boston
State of Massachusetts
N. America

prepaid

Milltown 29ᵗʰ October 1848

My dear Children
Your Letter of the 3ʳᵈ Instant reached us. We received the
amount of the order ye sent £9. Mʳ Quill the manager of
the National Bank in Tralee is a great friend of mine
otherwise I could not get as soon as I did. He de
=sired to have any future ₐorderₐ that may be sent us
drawn on the National Bank of Ireland and that It
should be paid without any delay. Your order
was a timely relief as we had the last of our store nearly
exhausted. Yet my dear Children, believe me we
feel greater pleasure on receiving assurance that ye
were in good health. May ₐGodₐ continue that blessing to
ye. We are well thank God. Your Mother is better than
this while past. Maurice and family are well. He returns
ye thanks for the portion ye sent him. He would be glad
to know whether Con received any of the two letters He
sent as he considered it his duty to thank Con more
than either of ye for the favours he received and which
he confesses to be the means preserving himself and

family. Michael's Wife and family are well. His[79] Children
are in good health and always with their Grandmother
and me from time to time as he always saw. I am ˄returning˄ thanks
to each of my children, and tell Julia that I thank
Con and her for £4 of the present order and Michael
for £5. James Maurice returns ye sincere thanks
and says he will be happy when ye call him out.
I believe and hope that his conduct and appearance will
reflect no discredit on ye. He is clever and well be
=haved. Ye desired to let ye know the state of the
country. It is bad in one respect. Distress is very
great. The blight swept off the potatoe crop and
this left provision short here. We have no sort
of employment for the poor, and the workhouses are
scarcely sufft to receive them. Farmers are oppressed
with poor rates and other charges. Many are deserting
their farms and flying to America as fast as they
can. Destitution is seen almost every where.
As for any disturbances, We know nothing of them
here. Our part of the country is as quiet as ever.
They had some meetings and speeches down the
country. Some of the leaders were apprehended
and tried. Some transported, others found guilty
of treason[80] and I suppose must suffer unless
the Crown extends mercy to them but I know
nothing of these affairs and ye may as
well never enquire of me about them.
Her Aunt Norry desired to be remembered to
Julia. She and her and daughter Catherine met us
yesterday in Tralee. They live at Feniat where

---

79. The word *His* is written over the word *the.*
80. James is referring to the Young Ireland Movement.

Catherine's Husband William Webb is stationed. They
are all well. Let us know if ye met Jude
Mahony in Boston. If ye know her there, tell her
that her Mother and Sisters want relief if she could
send it. I will only say that our blessing
is always for ye, and that I am
affectionately
your Father
James Prendergast

40. From James Prendergast to his children in Boston

Mr Thomas Prendergast
N° 16 Pearlplace
Boston
State of Massachusetts
N. America

prepaid
My Father last hand
last signature[81]

Milltown 15th Decr 1848

My dear Children
Last night's post brought me your Letter dated 2[. . .][82]
Novr and containing a check for £5 to Daniel Riordan. I was glad
to see that Con did not forget his Brother. I sent Daniel word

---

81. These two lines regarding the signature are written in pencil, probably by Thomas.
82. The numeral is smudged and illegible.

this day to be here on Thursday next and your ₌Mother₌ will go with him to Tralee on Friday when the check will be payable. I could enjoy no greater pleasure than to hear that my children are well. It added to my joy to hear from ye at present as I dreaded I should never have that pleasure, and I am sure It will be the last. When I sent the last letter in reply to the one ye sent the 3rd of October containing an Order for £9 I was unwell, but I did not choose to alarm ye, especially, as I expected to hear from ye in the course of a short time, and I hoped my illness would wear off. [. . .][83] In this I was mistaken. My malady encreased, and for the last six weeks I am confined to my bed. Thank God the priest attended to me a few days since. He and the Doctor say I cannot expect to hold out long. The only regret I feel in quitting this life is that of leaving your Mother alone, but I am reconciled to submit to the will of Heaven, as I know ye will not neglect her. I am sure ye may address the next letter to her as I think I will not live then. Ye may keep my illness from Julia as long as ye can and prepare her for the account by degrees.

Thanks to your goodness my dear Children I had every comfort hitherto, but now I am pennyless. The last of what I had is gone. A long illness in these times takes away money very quickly. If I die, as I am sure I will before many days, there is not a shilling in the House to defray my funeral expences, and your Mother must have recourse to credit from some neighbours until ye relieve her. The neighbours think so much of her and ye that I hope they will not refuse her. She is in as good health as strong as you saw her for some time past, were it not for the trouble she is undergoing during my sickness. Maurice was present at writing this. He attends me regularly in raising and

---

83. The letters are crossed out.

laying me on my bed. He and his family are in good health. Michael's Wife and Children and peopleinlaw are well. 3 of the children Julia James and John were unwell since November last but they are perfectly recovered now. His wife received a letter from him with a check for £11. I suppose he will receive a Letter from her immediately. My dear Children, as I ˄am˄ sure this will be the last from receive with it my paternal benediction. May the almighty and merciful God bless and protect ye. I offer this prayer for each and every of my children, not forgetting Con, the two Kates. My blessing attend ye always. I will say no more than that I am affectionately your Father

Ja[84]

James Prendergast

P.S.

I attempted to write my name and tho' I was supported by Maurice and your Mother I was unable to finish it. Nature is nearly exhausted. I then desired Danl Connell, who always writes for me, to put my name to it.

---

84. The attempted signature is shaky and smudged.

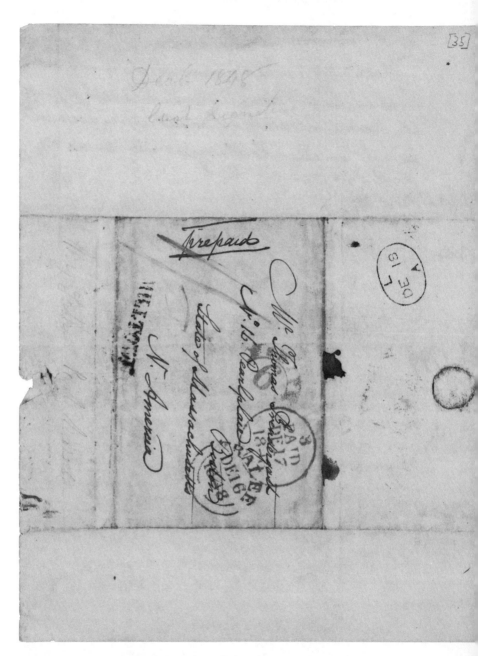

LETTER 40. James's final letter to his children in Boston. It was written three days before his death. The scrivener was Daniel Connell.

Milltown 15th Decr 1848

My dear Children

Last nights post brought one your Letter dated 2 ... and Containing a Check for £5 to Daniel Riordan. I was glad to see that Con did not forget his Brother. I sent Daniel word this day to be here on Thursday next and your Mother will go with him to Tralee on Friday when the Check will be payable. I could enjoy no greater pleasure than to hear that my Children are well It added to my Joy to hear from ye at present. as I dreaded I should never have that pleasure. And I am sure It will be the last. When I sent the last letter in Reply to the one ye sent the 3rd of October Containing an Order for £9. I was unwell. but I did not choose to alarm ye, especially, as I expected to hear from ye in the course of a short time. and I hoped my illness would wear off. In this I was mistaken. My Malady encreased. and for the last six Weeks I am Confined to my bed. Thank God the priest attended to me a few days since. He and the Doctor say I cannot expect to hold out long. The only Regret I feel in quitting this life is that of leaving your Mother alone. but I am reconciled to Submit to the Will of Heaven. as I know ye will not neglect her. I am sure ye may address the next Letter to her as I think I will not live then. Ye may keep my illness from Julia as long as ye can And prepare her for the account by degrees

Thanks to your goodness my dear Children I had every comfort hitherto. but now I am pennyless. the last of what is gone. a long illness in these times takes away Money so quickly. If I die as I am sure I will before many days. th... not a Shilling in the House to defray my funeral expense... your Mother must have recourse to credit from some Neigh... until Ye relieve her. The Neighbours think so much of... Ye that I hope they will not refuse her. She is in as go... health as strong as you saw her for some time past. were... for the trouble she is Undergoing during my sickness. Mauri... present at writing this. He attends me regularly in raising... laying me on my bed. He and his family are in good hea... Michael's Wife and Children. & people in law. are well. 3 of... Children. Julia James & John were unwell since November... but they are perfectly recovered now. His wife received a... from him with a check for £9. I suppose he will recei... Letter from her immediately. My dear Children. As I s... this will be the last from receive with it my paterna... benediction. May the Almighty & Merciful God bless a... protect Ye. I offer this prayer for each and every of m... Children, not forgetting Con, the two Kates. My blessin... Ye always. I will say no more than that I am...

Affectionately your...

James Prenderga...

P.S.

I attempted to write my name and tho' I was supported by Maurice and your Mother I was unable to finish it. nature is nearly exhausted. I then desired Dan Connell who always writes for me, to put my name to it

41. From Elizabeth Prendergast to her children in Boston

Mr Thomas Prendergast
N° 16 pearplace
Boston
State of Massachusetts
N. America

prepaid
My Mother[85]

Milltown 24th Decr 1848

My dear Children
This is the first letter I ever addressed
ye. I am sorry to be the only person
now able to address ye but the will
of God must done. We ought to be
obedient ˄to˄ his orders at all times. My
dear Children consider that all powers
must submit to God, and without his
blessing nothing can prosper. We must bear
our portion of Adversity, as well as we
enjoy our comforts, blessed be God. I have
my own share of troubles tho I had
a good deal of comfort hitherto. The sole
cause of my trouble is the painful duty
of announcing to ye the death of your father.
He died on the evening of Monday the 18th
Instant. Tho he had a long sickness It was
not painful. Nature only wasted gradually.
I was as well able to attend him as when
at the age 20. He wanted no care. His

---

85. The words *My Mother* are written in pencil, probably by Thomas.

daughterinlaw Michael's Wife nursed ˄him˄ as
carefully as any daughter could. Her own
father could expect no more. I had not
a single shilling to bury him but Nelly
said she had plenty and that she would
see ˄him˄ as respectably interred as if her Husband
were at home, and she fulfilled her Word.
He was interred in Keel alongside his son
John. Not a farmer in the parishes here
was attended to the grave with greater
respect, nor with greater decency than his
daughterinlaw sent him to his long home.
Ye should never forget her attention to
him nor will I during my life. She and her
children are well. The children are well tho
after a long fit of illness. Your Aunt Norry
and her daughter Mrs Webb were here a few
days before his death and came secondly the
Evening before his death. They asked me to go out
with them, but your father desired I would
keep my own little house during my life and
I intend doing as he desired me. Maurice attended
him regularly. He was here on the 15th (Milltown
fair day) when your father sent ye a letter with
his blessing which I am sorry to say he truly
to be his last. I now send every one of ye
[. . .]^{86} he did my blessing. I suppose tho I
am strong yet I cannot hold long. Time wears
every thing. I know I need not state that
I am now dependant on ye. I know ye will [not]
neglect repaying Nelly for what she laid
out for your father's funeral. She deserves

---

86. The paper is torn and the word is missing.

every attention. Maurice desires to be remembered
to ye. Poor fellow is in grief. He begs of me to request
that ye will keep Julia ignorant of her
father's death as long as possible. I am
My dear Children affectionately your
Mother Elizabeth Prendgast
Your Aunt Norry and family live at Feanit.[87]

42. From Elizabeth Prendergast to her children in Boston

Mr Jeffery Prendergast
69 Southstreet Boston
State of Massachusetts
N. America

T.S.P.

Milltown 10th November 1849

My dear Children
Yesterday I received the am^t of your Order, sent
in your letter of the 4th of October last[88]. Mr Quill, Director
of the ~~National~~ ˄Provincial˄ Bank is as good friend to me as he was
to your father. He said that he would always cash for me,
as often ~~as often~~ as I should want it, tho it was on
the National Bank no matter where when the order was
good. I need ˄not˄ say I am thankful for what ye send me at all
times and that I feel more pleasure on receiving an account
of the welfare of my children and their families than any
gift I could get myself. Thank God that ~~I am~~ ye ˄are˄ well. I am

---

87. This postscript is written in the left margin of the second page of the letter.
88. The word *last* is written over the word *next*.

well thank God and so are all the friends, Michael's Wife and
children and Maurice and Family. I received the am^t of the check
ye sent in may last and I returned an answer (I believe)
twice over. Michael's Wife received the am^t of her
order in due time and replied directly. I suppose he has
received it long before this. My dear Children It is un
=necessary for me to say that ˌI amˌ really sorry for what ye
lost by the failure of your employer, but it is useless to
despair. Ye could not foresee nor avoid it. Ye cannot
~~avoid it~~ ˌblame yourselvesˌ, therefore, do not fret too much. God is good
and will reward the honest man. May God
bless and help ye. I have one thing to tell ye.
Last year The Revd Mr Buckley published a
station here, and your father received him. He has
done the same now and will be with me
tomorrow, and if it cost £5 I would not
refuse receiving him. Reply to this as soon
as you can and tell how every one of ye and
and your families are situated and what Julia
and Con are doing. Maurice begs you will tell him
what particular trade James Maurice is bound
to. Tell James his mother is displeased for not
writing to her. She could expect nothing else yet.
They cannot understand what a Mechanist is
is in your Country, for here we call all good
tradesmen Mechanics. Tell Mich^l that his
Wife paid Mich^l Ginna the little that was due
to him. I will say only that I send my blessing to
each of ye young and old ~~and~~ not forgetting Con and Julia
and that I am affectionately
your Mother
Elizabeth Prendergast

43. From Elizabeth Prendergast to her children in Boston

Mr Jeffry Prendergast
69 South street Boston
State of Massachusetts
N. America

Milltown 21st Jany 1850

My dear Children
I replied to your letter of the 19th of Oct^r
last, and I was so well satisfied with the am^t
I then received that I was satisfied to await a
return, whenever it may be your convenience.
However I was much alarmed at the arri
=val of Father Batt OConnor who reached here
the day before yesterday. He made it his first
business to call on me and declare publickly
that ye were the best friends he met since He
left home. He spoke of some more in particular,
among whom was Batt Doyle. He said that all
his Countrymen shewed themselves as Irishmen
ought, his friends and friends to the cause on which
he went. He further informed me that Thomas
was in a delicate state of health, and that Jeffry's
Wife gave him a Pound to hand me on his arrival.
Of course, I am, and ought to be much obliged to
her, who never saw me and remembered me.
I fear much lest Thomas should be worse
than he said and I dread greatly that Jude
is not as she was and to say she did not join
Jeffry's Wife to be remembered to me. I well know
Con would be as willing as she would. He
always was and and your Father and I always
considered ‚him‚ as one of our own children and so

we ought. I am not in a good state of health this
time past, and I am nothing better now. I am very
proud to hear that Father Batt baptized a
for Jeffry a young James. May God bless him
and his parents and all my Children and families.
I will expect a reply to this without delay,
and to shew me that Thos is not in a very
bad state I expect he will write so that
I may know it. Maurice is here present at writing
this. He is like a madman. He fears His son is not
alive as He never wrote since he left home. He
says if his sons followed the example of his uncle
He would be more grateful. His poor mother is nearly
distracted. Sometime since, Maurice addressed you
on the subject. He was then in a state of distraction
somuch that ˄He˄ did not desire to be remembered to either
brother or sister, neither did he subscribe his name.
Father Batt did not make him much easier
as He says He only heard the lad was bound
[. . .]^{89} Trade but He does not say he saw him.
[. . .] your reply to this send every accoun[. . .]
that will make the poor man quiet. Tell the
truth. Say what the trade is. Maurice says He
is much surprized ˄he does not enquire as he knows how he left them˄ and
    Mich^{ls} Wife and Children
are all well. They would wish to hear from him oftener.
She is very careful and industrious to do the
most she can for the Children. I will only
say that I send all my children and their offspring
my blessing, and that I am affectionately
your Mother
Elizabeth Prendergast

---

89. The paper is damaged where the letter was sealed.

44. From Elizabeth Prendergast to her daughter Julia, and to her son Thomas

Mr Cornelius Riordan
72 Southstreet Boston
State of Massachusetts
N. America

Milltown 23rd Feby 1850

My dear Julia
Your Letter of the 5th Instant arrived here on
the 20th and I need not say that I ˄could˄ have no greater
pleasure than to hear that my Children are well and happy,
and I would feel equally happy to go and spend the rest of my
life with them whatever may be the danger or fatigue of
the Voyage But I have one reason for not attempting it and
I think you will deem me just. You know according
to the course of nature I cannot live long, and as I began
the world, when young, with your Father, I think I would act
unfairly If I did not wish to be buried with him. I have
no greater wish than enjoy a portion of the same grave. So my
dear child, I am fully determined to remain until that period
which of course cannot be very distant. I cannot complain
as I have good Children who never see me want, and I
will be careful of what they send me. I received the parcel
you sent from Father Batt with two snuff boxes and snuff and
I return you thanks for what you sent. I am sure I have
plenty of clothes during the rest of my life and I know I will
not want subsistence. Give my love to Con, to your Brothers
their Wives and Children and not forgetting James Maurice.
I will say no more than to send ye all
my blessing, praying that God may

protect and preserve ye, and I remain
affectionately, your Mother
Elizabeth Prendergast

To Thomas
My Dear Thomas
You see by my letter to Julia that your letter
of the 5th reached me. I return ye all thanks for the
kindness ye shew me and I trust I shall never forget
what ye do for me. I went to Father Batt and shewed
him your Letter. His reply was that he would give
me double the sum if you desired it. At the same
time when I told him my reason for not attempting
the voyage, He agreed with me in opinion. I am
sure I will never leave this place until I shall be
buried with your Father. I am sure I will get the
am^t of the check when it becomes payable. I will
be careful how to dispose of it. I have a parcel
of small socks to send the Children. I went to
Killorglin to see John Daly's daughter. She and
her family are well and her father said she would
not [. . .] ⁹⁰ this season. One of his neighbors told me
[. . .]s unlikely she would go at all as her parents
[. . .] provide for her at home. Father Batt told
[. . .] that Jeffry had a young son. I was
[. . .]h surprized that neither of ye mentioned
[. . .]ous letter. Send me every account about it.
[. . .] am very sorry to have to tell you that poor
Maurice was very unlucky with regard to the ch[. . .] ⁹¹
he rec^d from his son. The 3rd night after being paid the

---

90. The letter is torn and a section is missing.
91. The paper is damaged where the letter was sealed.

am^t some person came at night and took the Box
which contained £4 away. The Box was found broken
near the lake on the following morning. He suspects
a Boy of John Lynch's, John David Sullivan. James
knows him. He is a bad character. It left him bare
and poorly situated. Tell James Maurice he had every right
to enquire for his uncle Darby. His father and Grandmother were
so much ashamed that they would not shew his letter to his
uncle. I send ye all my blessing and remain affectionately
your Mother
Elizabeth Prendergast
P.S Tell Mich^l that his Wife and Children are well, and that his Wife is
much
surprized he does not write. I am ashamed myself to see him so careless.
He did not
even enquire for them in several letters that came here. What he sent
would not
support and clothe them, besides keeping th[. . .]ool,^{92} and that she does
regularly.
The death of her Mother is a great [. . .].^{93}

---

92. The letter is torn and a section is missing.
93. The postscript is written in the left margins of the second and third pages of the letter.

45. From Elizabeth Prendergast to her children in Boston, and from Maurice Prendergast to his son James Maurice

Mr Jeffrey Prendergast
69 Southstreet Boston
State of Massachusetts
N. America

Milltown 14th July 1850

My dear Children
I received your Letter of the 25th of June last bringing three checks
for £5 each and as you say it was very timely relief to each for whom they
were intended. I need not say what pleasure we enjoy when we hear
that ye are well. All your friends here are well. Michael's Wife and
Children are well and so are Maurice and family. As I suppose their own
    letters
will reach ye as soon as this I need say no more about them. I am in good
health thank God and I am sure I would be 15 years younger if I were once
with ye, and I hope I will soon enjoy that pleasure if ye send for me. I am
sure ye will think ₐitₐ strange to say I have changed my mind so soon, but I
will explain to you the reason. When last ye sent for me I was unwilling
to go that I may help Maurice who was then as I thought really distressed.
Now he is not so as his son sent him good relief thro the assistance of
his uncles. I pretended that I promised your father to be buried with
him, but now I must tell the truth, he never desired it. His last
words to me were that he would wish I should go to my children
and be under the eye of my daughter if I thought I could endure
the fatigue of the Voyage, but if I did not go he desired I should
be buried in Keel. I am sure I am strong and healthy enough and I
am sure I would get better from the thought of being going to
my children. Therefore I hope and request ye will send for me

as soon as possible while I have the fair weather and I will go
without delay. I can live with ye at less expense and with more comfort
to myself, for if ye sent me £5 every month I could save
nothing. Tell Julia I got the black allapacha[94] and second Mourning[95]
for which she inquired ˄for˄ together with the other articles which I
I named in a former letter. I expect ye will let me know
what I shall do to John's Orphan. I feel it a real hardship to part
her, however I will be governed by ye who are supporting her and
me. She is a good hardy girl about 8 years old. I mentioned her
in my former Letter and as it seems ye forgot saying any
thing about her I wish to mention the matter again for ye
to act as ye please. As to the news of the day here there
is no alteration since the last. We ˄have˄ no sort of employment and
      provisioning
that is to say indian meal is plentiful it is not easy to procure
it, as money is very scarce and nothing doing. I send my love and
blessing to each and every of my children and their families not forgetting
Con and Julia. Tell James Maurice I am thankful to him for enquir
=ring for me. I hope he is a good Boy and obedient to the advice
of his uncles and aunt. May God bless and preserve ye all
is the constant prayer of your affectionate Mother
Elizabeth Prendergast

My dear James
You can see by your Grandmothers letter that the three
checks sent by your uncles arrived here. They were very timely.
You ˄need˄ not say that it was the Gift of your uncle you sent me. I well
know without his assistance you could ˄send˄ me nothing yet
awhile. And tho I thank you for being the messenger, I thank your

---

94. Alpaca.
95. Second mourning: Mourning dress was commonly worn in the Victorian era. After a year or so in
    full mourning—wearing limited types of fabric and only the color black—came a period of second
    mourning, which lasted a shorter period and allowed a wider selection of fabrics and colors.

uncle for enabling you to do so. I need not say that I am happy
to hear that my Brothers and their families, Julia, Con and you are all
well. Your mother Brothers ~~and~~ sisters and myself are in good health
thank God. I left Dromin last may. I live at Ballyoughtra.
Mr Spring gave me the house in which Bowler lived, and the field
next the orchard to the rere of Shea's house for £2..10 for 12 months.
John Lynch treated me very badly as I had no person to prove our
agreem^t. He charged me for grazing the cow the same in Winter
as in summer and cheated me out ˄of˄ my labour as I had none to
to prove my work. He Decreed me at Killarney sessions for
three Pounds. If I remained with him and to give every little remit
=tance I could get from your uncles thro you we would never
disagree, but I could not bear to do that. If ˄I˄ remain where
I am for next year Mr Spring promised to give me the little
~~field~~ ˄strip˄ on the west side of the Road between Larry Dowd's House
and Knockreagh containing about 5 Acres. Your uncle Jeffry knows
the place well. Consult your uncles on that head and let
me know what they think of the matter. If they approve of
it ˄I will˄ act as they desire. If ye see Doctor Spring return him thanks
for the kindness of his family to me. I shall never forget it. His Brother
Mr William is one of my best friends. I would be very well if they
had any employment, but they only graze the land. You can hardly
believe what is thought of the last remittance sent by your uncles.
and [. . .]^96 there is more said of three checks sent together
[. . .] all they ever sent before. This country is very low.
Employment is totally done away here. You can see
this yourself when I tell you that Conny Cronin of Dromin
is the man who enquired for you at your uncles. If He had
employment at home he would not go out. I am sure your
uncle Mich^l will be glad to hear what I have to say of his family. They

---

96. The paper is damaged where the letter is sealed.

are very well. His children are as neatly kept and as well attended as
any in the neighbourhood, always at school and regular in their
conduct. They are promising to be strong healthy. James will
will make an able man. Tell your uncle Mich[l] that Norry Sheehy
Roger Sheehy of Clounmore's daughter is in real distress. Her Husband
Michael Moriarty went to america in 1847. She did not hear from
him for the last 12 months. If ye could learn where he is tell us
that she may write to him. Your mother Brothers and sisters join
me to send ye all our love and blessing. I remain affectionately your father
Maurice Prendergast
P.S. Tell your Uncle Con that Dan Riordan
is well and still in the Kenmare arms[97]

46. From Elizabeth Prendergast to her children in Boston

M[r] Cornelius Riordan
72 Southstreet Boston
State of Massachusetts
N. America

Milltown 7th August 1850

My dear Children
I suppose ye have received the last letter I sent
about the 8th of July last and that ye will be very
much surprized at receiving this so soon. But when
I explain the reason you will understand. I hope that
I am right. The blight came on early this season and

---

97. The postscript is written in the left margin of the second page of the letter.

it is thought the Potatoe crop is lost. In general
it is feared that this year will be worse than any
of the years past. Maurice had a large Garden
but is lost. What he and I laid out on it would buy
a great deal more than its produce. Now I
should be calling on ye always for relief and
after all I would not be the better for it as
I could make no reserve while any of my family
appeared distressed. So I will be much more
happy by living with ye, and it will cost ye less
to send me at once as much as will take me out
than to ˄be˄ always remitting me assistance. The
sooner ye send the better. I understand that
Mary Mahony (Tim^y Mahony's Widow) received
some Money from her daughters Judy and Nancy
who are in Boston, and that she, her young daugh
=ter, and her son are preparing to go out. In
that case I would be glad to be with
them, as I am sure they would take as
much care of me as any person could.
So the sooner you send for me the better. I
made the request in my last letter, therefore I will
only say now that it would come light between
ye. Maurice and his family are well. Michael's
Wife and family also. I am as well in health and
spirits, thank God, as I was within the last ten
years. I hope all my children and their families, as
well as if I named them individually, are happy and
in good health. Reply to this without delay
and let me how all of ye are. Do not forget Con or
Julia. I remain affectionately,
your Mother
Elizabeth Prendergast

P.S.

The enclosed note[98] is from your Aunt Norry.
It contains the address of her son, according to
the last account she had from him. He is out
from Ireland for the last 4 or 5 years. If ye
can learn any thing of him say so in your next.

---

98. The note is not extant.

*. . . what comforts I anticipate at the thoughts
of embracing each and every of you
so long parted from me.*

ELIZABETH PRENDERGAST,
August 1850

47. From Elizabeth Prendergast to her children in Boston

Mr Thomas Prendergast
79 Southstreet Boston
State of Massachusetts
N. America

Milltown 19th Augt 1850

My Dear Children
Just now, the Postboy handed me your letter of the 7th
Instant covering a check for £5. I need not say what joy
I feel when I hear that ye are all well, and how I am
more than joyful at the thoughts of being going to my dear
children. Figure to yourself what comforts I anticipate
at the thoughts of embracing each and every of you so long
parted from me. I have another cause of great pleasure
and joy namely your sending for John's little Orphan.
She is going from misery, and parting a tribe I never
liked. We are ready as soon as the Agent will call
on us. I hope we will be well prepared. I have a good
featherbed and plenty bedclothes to take with me, and ye
have sent me the means to procure the rest. I felt
so anxious to go out that I wrote a second letter after the
one you answered. I hope you will not be troubled
with replying to it as all my expectations are now
answered. I am very well in health and spirits
thank God. So are Maurice and his Family and
Michael's Wife and family. All your
friends are well. I called on father Batt.
He was out ˄of˄ home but I shewed your letter
to his cousin father Buckly who said he would
deliver your message. As I expect to see

ye all shortly I will only say that
I remain affectionately
your Mother
Elizabeth Prendergast
P.S.
Wm Dinneen called on me and begged that you
would tell Mich^l he requested of Mich^l to see his
son Edwd Dinneen, who lodges at David Kelly's
59 Ellis street, and to tell him that his father sold
what he had to go out as soon as he writes. W^m
wrote to him when I wrote to ye but received no
answer. He and his family are very anxious to sail
with me. He begs of Mich^l to say in his next whether
Edwd is married or not.

48. From Elizabeth Prendergast to her son Thomas

Thomas Penderg[...]^99
No 79 south street
Boston
North America

Liverp[...]^100

My Dear and Loving son Thom[...]^101
I tak this fa[...]^102
writing these few lines hoping to[...]

---

99. The letter is torn.
100. The letter's date is missing, but it is postmarked Liverpool, September 20, 1850.
101. The paper is damaged and the end of the name is missing.
102. The letter is torn.

Brothers and sisters and Con and [. . .]
good health as this leaves me and [. . .]
Riordan and Patrick Fitzgerald [. . .]
Thanks be to the Great God for all his [. . .]
and also Maurices family and Michaels wife and
family. Dear Thomas I wish to let you know that
we are here 7 days under heavy cost waiting until
the ship sails. Her name is Noibe [103] and her
captains name is Soule which is to Leave Liverpool
on the 21st instant. We have no account of the
Western star. I have to inform ye that there was
not 6 persons in the boat but fell sick from Cork to
Liverpool but myself which braved that much
[. . .] [104] well Thanks be to god
[. . .]lth and courage to cross the
[. . .]lso the rest of them
[. . .] say but we all join in one
[. . .]ends you all kind love and
[. . .] Loving mother until Death.
Elizabeth Pendergast
Florence Riordan wishes to be kindly
Remembered to his loving Brother and his
wife Julia and to all the Boys. May
the Blessing of God be with you all.

---

103. The correct spelling is *Niobe*.
104. The letter is torn.

LETTER 48. The final letter in the collection. It was sent by Elizabeth from Liverpool just before she embarked on her journey to Boston.

Liverp...

Dear and Loving Son Thom...

I take this pr...
...ting those few lines hoping...
...thers and sisters and Con and...
...d health as this leaves me and...
...ordan and Patrick Fitzgerald...
...nks be to the Great God for all th...
...also Maurices family and Michaels wife and...
...nily Dear Thomas I wish to let you know that...
...are here 7 days under heavy Cost waiting untill...
...ship sails her name is Noibe and her...
...tain name is Soule which is to Leave Liverpool...
the 21st instant we have no account of the...
...tern star I have to inform ye that there was...
...6 persons in the boat but fell sick from Cork to...
...rpool but myself which braved that much

...y well Thanks be to you

...lth and Courage to Cross the

...lso the Rest of them

...day but we all Join in o...

...nds you all Kind love And

...Loving Mother Untile Death

Elizabeth Pendergast

"N Florence Riordan wishes to be Kindly
Remembered to his loving Brother and his
wife Julia and to all the Boys may
the Blessing of God be with you all

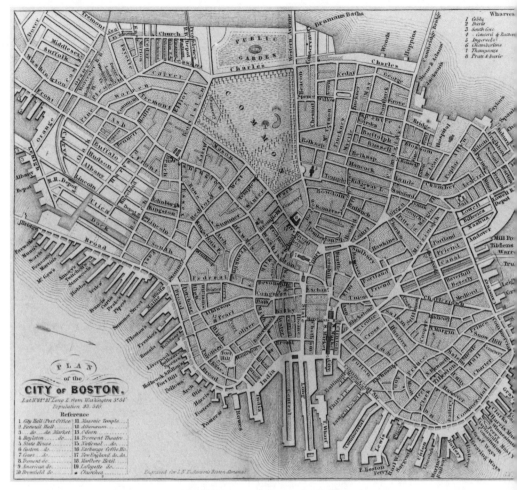

Plan of the City of Boston. (S. N. Dickinson, *Boston Almanac for the Year 1843*
[Boston: Thomas Groom])

The Prendergast Family in America

MARIE E. DALY

*T*HE FIRST-GENERATION Prendergast siblings came to America in the pre-Famine and Famine period, and settled along Boston's waterfront. Although they worked in low-wage jobs, they saved enough money eventually to purchase real estate while supporting family members in Ireland throughout the Famine. They were active socially, and occupied positions of leadership in Boston's Irish American community. They contributed their energy and funds to Catholic and Irish American causes. Although the first-generation Prendergasts were never wealthy, they were able to leave modest estates to their children.

Many of the second-generation Prendergasts did not follow the stereotypical pattern of Irish immigrants—obtaining secure but limiting employment—but chose to enter the business world as entrepreneurs. Their elevated economic and social status contradicts the stereotypical image of the Boston Irish as laborers, longshoremen, ward bosses, and tavern keepers. Their success in navigating the stratified society of nineteenth- and early twentieth-century Boston is notable, and bears further investigation. The success of the Prendergasts in Boston casts a new and interesting light on the history of the Irish in the Brahmin society of Boston. Intellectually gifted, several members of this second generation catapulted into the upper echelons of Irish American society, and even into Boston's higher social strata. They chose entrepreneurial careers as brokers, real estate agents, and insurance agents. They sat on the boards of well-known corporations. They joined elite social clubs and country clubs, and vacationed in the upscale beach communities of Nantasket and Hyannis Port. They remained devoutly Catholic, and, like their parents, they contributed funds and energy to various Catholic institutions and churches.

When the Prendergasts began arriving in Boston in 1840, the city was not hospitable to Irish immigrants. In the previous decade anti-Catholic riots had rocked the streets of the waterfront district.[1] Lacking education and skills,

---

1. Jack Tager, *Boston Riots: Three Centuries of Social Violence* (Boston: Northeastern University Press, 2000), 120–122.

rural Irish peasants could find little skilled employment and took jobs as seasonal general laborers, digging ditches, laying railroads, and constructing streets. They settled in the crowded and unsanitary waterfront areas where they could obtain cheap housing. In 1850, 23,000 people, one-half of whom were Irish immigrants and their families, lived in "tottering rookeries," in the "vicious slum" of Fort Hill.[2] When Thomas and Jeffrey arrived, they first lived in the Fort Hill district with their sister Julia and her husband—probably squeezed together into small, dark, and dank flats or cellars in their various rented residences on Oliver Street, Atkinson Street, and Pearl Place. Thomas obtained employment in the livery stable of Isaac Foster on Devonshire Street, until Foster went bankrupt in 1849.[3] Many members of the family had jobs involving horses and transportation—Thomas as a coachman, Jeffrey as a stabler, Michael as a harness cleaner, and Michael's sons as harness makers. By 1847, they had moved into the South Cove district, a recently filled waterfront area that was the locus of several railroad terminals.[4] In the next decade, brothers Michael and Jeffrey (and then Jeffrey's heirs), purchased buildings on South Street and Albany Street. These locations near busy railroad terminals provided the family with opportunities to make money.

Despite their parents' concern about their health, all the siblings but Jeffrey lived to old age. Their mother, Elizabeth (Hurley) Prendergast, emigrated with her son John's orphaned daughter Elizabeth in 1850. She died at age 87[5] on 15 March 1857 and was buried at Cambridge Catholic Cemetery on Saint Patrick's Day of that year.

Children of James Prendergast and Elizabeth Hurley

John	[?]–1847	m. Margaret Walsh
Maurice	ca. 1798–1874	m. Mary Sullivan
Michael	1805–1878	m. Ellen Roach
Julia	ca. 1812–1893	m. Cornelius Riordan
Jeffrey	1817–1859	m. Catherine Conway
Thomas	1820–1895	m. 1st Catherine Cotter
		m. 2nd Catherine Leary

---

2. Walter Muir Whitehill and Lawrence W. Kennedy, *Boston: A Topographical History*, 3rd ed. (Cambridge: Belknap Press of Harvard University Press, 2000), 174.

3. Letter #42, 10 November 1849.

4. Whitehill and Kennedy, *Boston*, 104.

5. Massachusetts Vital Records, 113:19.

John Prendergast and Margaret Walsh

John Prendergast was born in County Kerry, date unknown, and died before 21 April 1847.[6] He married Margaret Walsh on 7 January 1840 in Tralee.[7] Little is known about John and his family since he did not emigrate and died in Ireland in 1847, leaving his orphaned daughter Elizabeth in the care of her grandmother, Elizabeth (Hurley) Prendergast.

CHILDREN OF JOHN PRENDERGAST AND MARGARET WALSH

Julia Prendergast	1840–[?]
Elizabeth Prendergast	1843–[?]

Maurice Prendergast and Mary Sullivan

Maurice Prendergast was born about 1798 in County Kerry. According to the baptismal records of his children, he lived in Ardagh until 1842; after that he lived in Dromin, in the parish of Aghadoe, north of Killarney. He was probably the Maurice Prendergast who emigrated with a female named Eliza on the steamship *Malta* from Liverpool, arriving in Boston on 28 August 1872.[8] Presumably his wife had died in Ireland. He died on 16 March 1874 at 10 Leeds Street in Washington Village, South Boston,[9] at the residence of his sister Julia Riordan, which was adjacent to his brother Thomas's residence. Maurice's children were all born in Ireland, and their baptism records in Killarney indicate that his wife's name was Mary Sullivan.

CHILDREN OF MAURICE PRENDERGAST AND MARY SULLIVAN

James Maurice	1832–1902	m. Mary Holly
Jeffrey	1837–[?]	
Elizabeth	1840–[?]	
Julia	1842–[?]	
Thomas	1844–[?]	
Maurice	1846–[?]	
John	1848–1914	
Elizabeth	1850–1933	m. William Connell

---

6. Letter #29, 21 April 1847.
7. Marriages, Roman Catholic Church, Tralee, County Kerry, Ireland, 7 January 1840.
8. Passenger Arrival Lists, Port of Boston, August 1872.
9. Massachusetts Vital Records, 267:53; obituary, *Pilot,* 28 March 1874.

In letters sent to Boston, James Prendergast urged his sons to take in their brother Maurice's son James Maurice so that he could learn a trade. Young James Maurice was in Boston, living with his uncles, by 1849. In 1880, a 45-year-old James Prendergast, machinist, was living with his wife Mary and father-in-law, Patrick Holly, in North Cambridge, Massachusetts. The 1900 census indicated that he was a widower who had been married for thirty years, with no children, and who had emigrated in 1854 [sic]. In 1900, James Maurice lived with his siblings, John and Elizabeth, at 10 Dromey Street, Roxbury.[10] He died in Boston on 30 September 1902, and was buried at Calvary Cemetery.[11]

John Prendergast was born in Dromin, County Kerry, on 9 July 1848 or 12 March 1850, depending on the source.[12] He arrived in Boston in May 1866 or 1867. In the spring of 1871, he joined the U.S. Navy, serving for three years each on the ship *Wabash* and the monitors *Ajax* and *Richmond.* He became a naturalized citizen of the United States on 15 February 1882.[13] He joined the Boston Fire Department in July of that year, initially serving as a substitute fireman in Ladder Company 8, though he soon moved to a permanent position in Ladder Company 14.[14] John never married, and lived with his brother James and sister Elizabeth Connell in Roxbury in 1900. Ten years later, he was living with Elizabeth at 15 Glendale Street, Dorchester, and was assigned at that time to Ladder Company 4 at 198 Dudley Street in Roxbury.[15] He died on 7 June 1914.[16]

Elizabeth M. Prendergast emigrated to Boston with her father, arriving on the *Malta* on 28 August 1872.[17] She and her father lived with her aunt Julia Riordan at 10 Leeds Street, Washington Village, South Boston, and in the 1880 census Elizabeth was listed as a dressmaker. On 12 April 1882, Elizabeth married William J. Connell, a gardener from Lynn, who had been born in

---

10. 1900 Federal Census, Ward 16, Roxbury, ED #1395, sheet 14, line 28.

11. Massachusetts Vital Records, 531:324.

12. Albert Casey, *O'Kief, Coshe Mang, Slieve Lougher, and Upper Blackwater Ireland,* vol. 8, *Historical and Genealogical Items Relating to North Cork and East Kerry* (Birmingham, Eng.: Knocknagree Historical Fund, 1965), 1407; U.S. Circuit Court Boston Naturalization Petition, 139:3.

13. U.S. Circuit Court Boston Naturalization Petition, 139:3.

14. Arthur Wellington Brayley, *The Complete History of the Boston Fire Department, Including the Fire Alarm Service and the Protective Department, from 1630 to 1888* (Boston: J. P. Dale, 1889), 446.

15. 1910 U.S. Federal Census, Boston, ED 1264, sheet 24A, line 17; 1900 U.S. Federal Census Vol. 46, ED 845, sheet 8, line 76.

16. Boston City Directory, 1915, p. 1597.

17. Passenger Arrival Lists, Port of Boston, August 1872.

Boston Fire Department Ladder Companies 8 and 14, ca. 1888. Figure 5 is John Prendergast (Maurice's son). (Arthur Wellington Brayley, *A Complete History of the Boston Fire Department, Including the Fire–Alarm Service and the Protective Department, From 1630 to 1888* [Boston: J. P. Dale, 1889], p. 447)

Concord, the son of James and Catherine Connell.[18] William Connell died before 1900, and the couple was childless (Elizabeth was listed in 1900 as a widow with no children, living with her brothers in Roxbury.) In 1910, she lived with her brother John in Dorchester. Elizabeth died in Brookline on 27 April 1933.[19]

Michael Prendergast and Ellen Roach

Michael Prendergast was born in October 1805 according to his naturalization petition, but census documents place his birth around 1810. He married in Ireland Ellen Roach, born in 1812, the daughter of David and Julia Roach.[20] Michael and Ellen's children were all born in Ireland. On 27 March 1847, Michael set off on foot for Cork, and after a few days sailed for Saint John, New Brunswick. The *Cork Examiner* (5 April 1847) reported the scene at the docks at the time Michael left. "The quays are crowded every day with the peasantry from all quarters of the country, who are emigrating to America, both direct from this port, and 'cross channel' to Liverpool, as the agents here cannot produce enough of ships to convey the people from this unhappy country."[21] Three ships from Cork bearing passengers, the *Pallas,* the *Inconstant,* and the *Mary,* arrived in Saint John in May 1847, after voyages of fifty days each.[22] Michael probably emigrated on one of these three ships, possibly the *Mary.*[23] He probably arrived there in May 1847, but his journey onward to Boston was delayed by several weeks.

Overwhelmed with sick, starving Irish emigrants, Saint John authorities required that sick immigrants be quarantined on Partridge Island until their

---

18. Massachusetts Vital Records, 336:63.
19. Brookline, Massachusetts, City Directory, 1934, p. 86.
20. On Ellen's death record in Boston, her parents are listed as David and Julia Roach. Massachusetts Vital Records, 366:67.
21. Extract from the *Cork Examiner,* 5 April 1847, "An Gorta Mor: The Great Irish Famine, Homepage": http://www.swan.ac.uk/history/teaching/teaching%20resources/An%20Gorta%20Mor/news papers/cork%20examiner/ceapr47.htm.
22. "Ship Arrivals at the Port of Saint John, 1847: May," http//www.theshipslist.com/; J. Elizabeth Cushing, Teresa Casey, and Monica Robertson, *A Chronicle of Irish Emigration to Saint John, New Brunswick, 1847* (Saint John: New Brunswick Museum, 1979).
23. Saint John almshouse records indicate a number people from the *Mary* were from Kerry, whereas passengers from the *Pallas* and *Inconstant* were from Cork. Daniel F. Johnson, *The St. John County Alms and Work House Records* (Saint John: D. F. Johnson, 1985); Peter D. Murphy, *Poor Ignorant Children: Irish Famine Orphans in Saint John, New Brunswick* (Halifax, N.S.: D'Arcy McGee Chair of Irish Studies, Saint Mary's University, 1999).

health improved. The conditions on Partridge Island were dismal, with many of the sick forced to lie in tents or on the open ground. His brothers in Boston received a letter from Michael in New Brunswick, written 7 June. He may have spent some time in quarantine on Partridge Island before being allowed to proceed to Boston, where he arrived on 1 July 1847, according to his naturalization petition.[24] The delay of his arrival in Boston caused some consternation in his parents, who had heard of others dying during voyages to North America.

Michael left his wife Ellen and their four children in Milltown, and they did not emigrate until 1851 or 1852. In the 1850 census, he was living with his brother Thomas and family. He eventually settled on South Street, on land formerly owned by the Old Colony Railroad, between Kneeland Street and Beach Street in a neighborhood called the South Cove or Leather district. Although the city directories and census records listed his occupation as laborer or harness cleaner, he was able to amass enough capital to purchase real estate. He bought two buildings on South Street, the first purchased in 1861 from the Boston businessman and philanthropist Andrew Carney, and the second purchased in 1864.[25] At his death in 1878, the two duplex buildings at 184–186 and 190–192 South Street were valued at $6,500 each.[26] Michael died on 26 January 1878 at age 68, according to his death certificate.[27] Ellen outlived her husband and can be found in the 1880 census still living on South Street, next door to her daughter, Julia Foley. Ellen died on 6 March 1885 at 182 South Street.[28]

CHILDREN OF MICHAEL PRENDERGAST AND ELLEN ROACH

Mary	[?]–1843	
Julia	ca. 1838–1906	m. William Foley
James	1840–[?]	
James	1842–[?]	
James T.	1843–1903	m. Catherine O'Brien
Elizabeth	1844–ca.1879	
John	1846–1898	m. Catherine Anderson

---

24. U.S. District Court, 7:170.
25. Suffolk County Deeds, 798:315, 849:281.
26. Suffolk County Probate Records, Docket #61012.
27. Massachusetts Vital Records, 303:38.
28. Massachusetts Vital Records, 366:67.

Julia Prendergast was born around 1838 in Ireland, and probably emigrated with her mother in 1851 or 1852. On 4 November 1854, she married William Foley, born in Ireland in 1837, the son of John and Mary Foley.[29] The couple ran a grocery store in one of the buildings owned by Julia's parents. The 1870 census indicates that William Foley was a citizen of the United States. He died on 12 March 1875 at age 37 years.[30] Julia continued to live at the South Street address until after the death of her mother in 1885. She later moved to 86 Mount Pleasant Avenue in Roxbury, where she died on 5 January 1906. She was buried in Calvary Cemetery, Boston.[31]

James T. Prendergast was born on 7 December 1843 in Ireland (according to his naturalization petition), probably in Milltown, Co. Kerry. He arrived at South Boston on 15 July 1852.[32] He was a harness maker for many years, and worked at Byron Street, at the base of Beacon Hill. On 18 May 1871 in Boston, he married Catherine O'Brien, age 26, the daughter of Cornelius and Catherine O'Brien.[33] For most of his married life, he lived in Malden, Massachusetts; in 1900 he lived at 60 Granville Avenue in Malden. Like his brother John, his occupation at the time of his death was retired real estate agent. He and Catherine did not have any children. He died in Malden on 30 August 1903. He was buried alongside his brother John in Calvary Cemetery.[34]

Not much is known about Michael and Ellen's daughter Elizabeth. In Michael's will in 1878, she is listed as residing in New Orleans. The 1880 census does not list any Elizabeth Prendergast living there, though, and by 1882 a deed of Michael's estate listed her as deceased.

John Prendergast was born on 7 May 1846 (according to his naturalization petition and death record), probably in Milltown, Co. Kerry. He arrived in Boston on 15 July 1851.[35] From 1868 to 1884, he worked as a photographer on Washington Street and Tremont Row, and was in business for a few years in the 1870s with a Maurice Prendergast, who may have been his cousin.[36] By the time of his death in 1898, he was listed as a real estate agent. He married Cath-

29. Massachusetts Vital Records, 155:103.
30. Massachusetts Vital Records, 276:64.
31. Massachusetts Vital Records, 5:127.
32. U.S. District Court Boston Naturalization Petition, 45:8.
33. Massachusetts Vital Records, 237:76.
34. Massachusetts Vital Records, 35:205; 1900 U.S. Federal Census, vol. 46, ED 845, sheet 8, line 76.
35. U.S. District Court Boston Naturalization Petition, 48:261.
36. Chris Steele and Ronald Polito, *A Directory of Massachusetts Photographers, 1839–1900* (Camden, Me.: Picton Press, 1993).

erine Anderson sometime in the 1860s. She had been born in St. John, New Brunswick, in 1850 and was the daughter of Denmark native Peter Anderson and Irish-born Catherine Collace.[37] In 1880, the couple lived at 1 Byron Street, Beacon Hill. John had purchased the building with his brother James. Catherine died on 10 September 1893 at the age of 43, of chronic catarrhal inflammation of the lungs, which had affected her for years. At the time of her death, the couple was living at 25 Appleton Street in the South End.[38] The couple was childless, but in 1889 they took in an 8-year-old orphan girl, Jane (Jennie) Colgan, who was born in Boston on 2 October 1881, the daughter of New Brunswick natives Richard and Alma E. (Jane) Colgan (or McColgan).[39] John legally adopted the girl on 10 November 1898, one month before his death.[40] He died of tuberculosis on 3 December 1898 at his home on Appleton Street, at the age of 52.[41] At the time of his death, his estate was valued at over $18,000. He owned property at 16 Tyler Street, 26 and 27 Lawrence Street, 25 Appleton Street, and 1 Byron Street. In his will he left $1,000 to his brother James, the executor of his will, and $100 to his sister, Julia Foley. The residue of his estate was left in trust to his adopted daughter Jane, until she reached the age of 23 years.[42]

Julia Prendergast and Cornelius Riordan

Julia was born about 1812 and married Cornelius Riordan, the son of Cornelius and Mary Riordan, in Killarney on 8 November 1834.[43] Many of the early letters are addressed to Cornelius Riordan, and the two Prendergast brothers probably roomed with Julia and Cornelius until their marriages in 1846 and 1847. In 1850, Julia and Cornelius were living on South Street near her brother Jeffrey. Julia and Cornelius later moved to 10 Leeds Street in the Washington Village section of South Boston near her brother Thomas. Cornelius died there of pneumonia at the age of 58 on 16 February 1869.[44] Julia never remar-

37. Massachusetts Vital Records, 438:373.
38. Massachusetts Vital Records, 438:373.
39. Massachusetts Vital Records, 324:48.
40. Suffolk County Probate Records, Docket #109225.
41. Massachusetts Vital Records, 483:528.
42. Suffolk County Probate Records, Docket #109434, 789:196.
43. Albert Casey, *O'Kief, Coshe Mang, Slieve Lougher and Upper Blackwater Ireland*, vol. 5, *Historical and Genealogical Items Relating to North Cork and East Kerry* (Birmingham, Eng.: Knocknagree Historical Fund, 1962), 246.
44. Massachusetts Vital Records, 222:27.

ried. In 1872, her brother Maurice and his daughter Elizabeth came from Ireland and lived with her on Leeds Street. Maurice Prendergast died there in 1874. Julia died on 19 July 1893 at age 84 years.[45] She left an estate of about $1,000, most of which was cash in the Suffolk Savings Bank. She divided her estate between her brother Thomas and her brother Maurice's children, James Maurice and Elizabeth.[46]

Jeffrey Prendergast and Catherine Conway

Jeffrey Prendergast was born on 7 May 1817 (according to his parents, in letters #20 and #21). He emigrated as a young man with his brother Thomas, and arrived in New York City on 28 May 1840. He initially lived with Julia and Cornelius Riordan, his sister and brother-in-law, in the Fort Hill section of Boston. He was naturalized at the U.S. District Court in Boston on 9 November 1846, and his naturalization was witnessed by John S. Tyler and Isaac Foster, the employer of his brother Thomas.[47] Indeed, Jeffrey may have also worked for Foster, whose livery stable was located on Devonshire Street. (In letter #42, his mother consoles all of her children, not just Thomas, on what they lost by the failure of their employer.) Later, in an 1860 deed, Jeffrey's occupation was listed as stabler. He married Catherine Conway on 3 May 1847 at St. Patrick's Church in the South End. She was born on 1 May 1819 in Gortnahoe, Co. Tipperary, the daughter of Thomas Conway and Mary Hines.[48] (Jeffrey's father comments about the marriage and Catherine's birthplace in letter #32.) Jeffrey and Catherine moved to 69 South Street probably in 1849, and lived next door to Cornelius and Julia Riordan. (South Street was later renumbered to reflect the growth of population along it, and the building that Michael ended up owning in 1878 may have been the same as his brother Thomas's former residence at 90 South Street. Jeffrey and Catherine moved to 41 (later 51) Albany Street, between Kneeland and Harvard Streets, between 1856 and 1859. At an auction, he placed a bid for the building, a brick townhouse, and signed a purchase and sale agreement on 5 April 1859. He died before the sale went through, and the property was subsequently purchased by his estate

---

45. Massachusetts Vital Records, 438:289.
46. Suffolk County Probate Records, 675:20.
47. U.S. District Court Boston Naturalization Petition, 1:124.
48. Pedigree chart of James Maurice Prendergast, New England Historic Genealogical Society; Saint Patrick's Roman Catholic Church, Marriages 1836–1884, p. 64.

(Catherine and children) for $4,850.[49] Jeffrey died a relatively young man of 39 years, on 2 May 1859, of a skin infection.[50] He was buried on 4 May 1859 in one of Thomas's two lots in Cambridge Catholic Cemetery. There was no will or estate administration. His wife Catherine is shown in Bromley's 1890 *Atlas of Boston* still owning the building at 51 Albany Street,[51] but in the 1880 census she was living with her son James Maurice at 148 West Concord Street in the South End. She died at the age of 90 at the family's home at 135 Bay State Road, Boston, on 24 January 1909.[52] Owing to the wealth and prominence of her son James Maurice, her funeral Mass was celebrated at Holy Cross Cathedral by Archbishop William O'Connell, who was assisted by Rev. Thomas Gasson, S.J., president of Boston College. A large number of priests attended the funeral, as reported in the *Pilot* newspaper. She was buried at Calvary Cemetery in Boston on 27 June 1909.[53]

CHILDREN OF JEFFREY PRENDERGAST AND CATHERINE CONWAY

James	1848–[?]	
Mary Ellen	1850–1914	m. John Falvey
James Maurice	1851–1920	
Thomas	1854–[?]	
Elizabeth	1856–1857	
Julia Catherine	1859–1943	

Mary Ellen Prendergast was born in 1850, probably at 90 South Street, Boston. On 21 January 1875, she married John Falvey, who was born in Boston in 1843, the son of Michael and Margaret Falvey.[54] In 1880, the couple lived with Mary Ellen's mother, brother, and sister at 148 West Concord Street in the South End. Her husband died sometime before 1910, at which time she lived with her five children at 36 Perrin Street in Roxbury, about six blocks from Thomas and Maurice's children. In 1910, she had two live-in maids, and her occupation was listed as "own income."[55] She died in Boston in 1914. The

---

49. Suffolk County Deeds, 773:266.
50. Massachusetts Vital Records, 131:26.
51. George W. and Walter S. Bromley, *Atlas of the City of Boston* (Philadelphia: G. W. Bromley & Co., 1890), plate 9.
52. Massachusetts Vital Records, 7:89.
53. Obituary, *Pilot*, 30 January 1909.
54. Massachusetts Vital Records, 273:5.
55. 1910 U.S. Federal Census, Ward 21, Precinct 6, ED1555, sheet 2A.

Falveys' son Charles Anthony is said to have encouraged fellow Brookline, Massachusetts, resident Joseph P. Kennedy to consider choosing the Cape Cod community of Hyannis Port as the location of his family's summer home, assuring Kennedy of admittance to the Hyannis Port Country Club, which included numerous Catholics among its members.[56] The Falveys had five children, and numerous descendants live in Massachusetts, New York, and Hawaii.

James Maurice Prendergast was born on 29 October 1851 at 69 South Street, Boston.[57] He attended the old Josiah Quincy School on Tyler Street and Boston English High School in the public school system, and was twice awarded the Franklin certificate, an academic award for scholarship and conduct. At age 17, he went to work for Francis E. Bacon, a Boston cotton broker. He rose from the position of clerk to head of the firm, which was afterward named J. M. Prendergast & Co., located at 87 Milk Street. He was on the board of directors of several well-known Massachusetts corporations, including the Boston Elevated Railroad Corp., the Boston and Maine Railroad, the Hamilton Woolen Company, the New England Trust Company, the Second National Bank (vice president) and the Commonwealth Trust Company. He was also associated with the Brooklyn Electric Light Company in New York.[58] He was a member of the Boston Parks Commission for thirteen years, and was partly responsible for the expansion of the city's park system. In 1889, he was listed among the heaviest taxpayers in the Irish American community in Boston; his real estate was valued at $8,500 and his personal estate at $90,000.[59]

James Maurice was prominent in the Republican Party, and in 1907 refused an opportunity to run for mayor. He was active in charitable organizations, especially the Boston Association for the Relief and Control of Tuberculosis. In 1909, he donated to the association twenty acres of land; the hospital subsequently built there, named the Prendergast Preventorium, was located at 1000 Harvard Avenue, Mattapan. He donated to various Catholic charities and corresponded frequently with Cardinal O'Connell. He was a member of the

---

56. Ronald Kessler, *The Sins of the Father: Joseph P. Kennedy and the Dynasty He Founded* (New York: Warner Books, 1996), 40.
57. Massachusetts Vital Records, 53:72.
58. "... and Mr. James Prendergast, the well-known cotton-cloth commission merchant, were associated with Mr. Hern in the Brooklyn venture, and the company, among others things, secured the contract for lighting the streets of Brooklyn and the Brooklyn Bridge." James Bernard Cullen, ed., *The Story of the Irish in Boston* (Boston: James B. Cullen & Co., 1889), 418.
59. Cullen, *Story of the Irish*, 429.

Republican, Manhattan, Catholic, New Riding, Algonquin, Eastern Yacht, Boston Press, and Boston Country clubs, and the Boston Athletic Association. He and his sister Julia were also members of the New England Historic Genealogical Society.[60]

Over his lifetime he had a number of residences. As a young man he lived with his mother on South Street and Albany Street. By 1880, he had moved to 148 West Concord Street in the South End. By 1900, he lived at 135 Bay State Road.[61] According to descendants of Mary Ellen (Prendergast) Falvey, in the 1890s he began summering in Hyannis Port, Cape Cod, on Irving Avenue, where he owned a substantial house overlooking Nantucket Sound.[62] He also collected fine art during the 1890s. He never married, but remained close to his mother, siblings, and extended Prendergast family. With his elevated social and economic position, he was able to help his nephews secure employment in the various corporations with which he was connected. He died on 29 November 1920 at his home on Bay State Road.[63]

Julia Catherine Prendergast was born on 2 November 1859 at 41 Albany Street, Boston.[64] Her father had died six months before her birth. She remained at home with her mother and brother James Maurice all her life. She was educated in the Boston public schools and at Notre Dame Academy in Boston. Although she did not work, she was socially active and "belonged to many organizations, being an officer in the League of Catholic Women, Guild of the Infant Saviour and Boston Tuberculosis Association and the Women's Republican Club of Boston."[65] When her family moved to 135 Bay State Road, she accompanied them, and also summered with them at Hyannis Port. She inherited the estate of her wealthy brother, James Maurice, and subsequently made bequests to the Prendergast Preventorium (founded by her brother), Carney Hospital, the Society for the Propagation of the Faith (a Catholic missionary society), the Little Sisters of the Poor, the House of Good Shep-

60. Obituary, *Boston Globe*, 30 November 1920; *Men of Massachusetts* (Boston: Boston Press Club, 1903); Albert Nelson Marquis, ed., *Who's Who in New England* (Chicago: Albert Nelson Marquis & Co., 1916), 873.

61. 1880 U.S. Federal Census, vol. 30, ED722, p.203C; 1900 U.S. Federal Census, ED1329, p. 6.

62. Paul Fairbanks Herrick and Larry G. Newman, *Old Hyannis Port, Massachusetts: An Anecdotal, Photographic Panorama* (New Bedford: Reynolds-DeWalt, 1968), 10.

63. Obituary, *Boston Globe*, 30 November 1920; Massachusetts Vital Records, 24:465.

64. Massachusetts Vital Records, 125:119; Saint James Roman Catholic Church, Baptisms 1854–1864, p. 195.

65. William Carroll Hill, "Memoirs of Deceased Members of the New England Historic Genealogical Society," *New England Historical & Genealogical Register*, 98 (1944): 82-83.

herd orphanage, the St. Vincent de Paul Society of the Holy Cross Cathedral, the Home for Destitute Catholic Children, and St. Vincent's Orphan Asylum. In addition, she donated fifteen paintings to the Museum of Fine Arts in memory of her brother. Among them are Claude Monet's *Entrance to the Village of Vetheuil in Winter*, Jean-Victor Bertin's *Entrance to the Park at Saint-Cloud*, Constant Troyon's *Fox in a Trap*, and Leon-Augustin Lhermitte's *Wheatfield (Noonday Rest)*.[66] Julia died in Hyannis Port on 21 September 1943. Her funeral was held from her home on Irving Avenue, and the funeral Mass at St. Francis Xavier Church in Hyannis Port. She was buried at Calvary Cemetery in Boston.[67]

Thomas Prendergast, Catherine Cotter, and Catherine M. Leary

Thomas Prendergast was born on 29 May 1820 in Milltown, Co. Kerry, according to his father and his naturalization petition. Thomas was the only one of the brothers who was literate when he emigrated, although Cornelius Riordan likely was also literate, since many of the letters were addressed to him. He emigrated from Ireland on 28 May 1840 to New York City with his brother Jeffrey, and became a naturalized citizen on 9 November 1846 in the U.S. District Court of Boston.[68] He worked for Isaac Foster, who had a livery stable on Devonshire Street. He married Catherine Cotter on 2 September 1846 in Saint Patrick Church, in the South End.[69] She died on 6 January 1855 in Boston, at age 31 years, of inflammation of the lungs, and was buried at Cambridge Catholic Cemetery.[70] By the end of 1856, Thomas had married a second time, to Catherine M. Leary, daughter of Daniel Leary (O'Leary) and Mary Connell. They lived first at 90 South Street and then at 41 Albany Street, until 1865, when he purchased land on Leeds Street in the Washington Village section of South Boston.[71] For Thomas and his family, moving to this neighborhood was a step up, since the area had a more spacious and suburban feel, even if the narrow townhouse did not. (As described in one contemporary ac-

---

66. Collections database, Museum of Fine Arts, Boston, http://www.mfa.org/artemis/.
67. *Register* 98 (1944): 82–83; obituary, *Cape Cod Standard-Times*, 22 September 1943; Massachusetts Vital Records, 4:192.
68. U.S. District Court Boston Naturalization Petition, 1:123.
69. Saint Patrick's Roman Catholic Church, Marriages 1836–1884, p. 58.
70. Massachusetts Vital Records, 85:2.
71. Suffolk County Deeds, 867:255.

Portrait of James Maurice Prendergast
(Jeffrey's son). (*Men of Massachusetts*
[Boston: Boston Press Club, 1903], p. 64)

Portrait of Daniel Leroy Prendergast
(Thomas's son). (*Men of Massachusetts*
[Boston: Boston Press Club, 1903)], p. 325)

Road's End, Hyannis Port, Massachusetts. The summer home of Jeffrey Prendergast's son
James Maurice Prendergast. (Photograph courtesy of Megan Newman)

count, "Leaving this crowded selvage of South Boston, the more open streets of Washington Village are followed, with frequent views over the South Bay on the right, and Boston Harbor on the left.")[72]

Thomas was active in several Irish American and Catholic societies, and rose to positions of leadership in some of them. As a member of the Shields Artillery Guards, an Irish American paramilitary organization disbanded by the Know-Nothings, he witnessed the Anthony Burns riots on State Street, as inflamed abolitionists tried to rescue a fugitive slave. He was an organizer and leader of a branch of the Father Mathew Temperance Society, and an organizer of the Ancient Order of Hibernians in Boston. Active in Catholic charitable organizations, he supported his church, Carney Hospital, and House of the Good Shepherd orphanage. He was an avid reader who donated his large collection of books to his church library.[73] On 28 April 1890, he and his family moved to 26 Brookford Street in Roxbury, just around the corner from his brother Maurice's children.[74] On 31 January 1895, at Brookford Street, he died of bronchitis at age 68 according to his death record (his actual age was probably 75 years).[75] In his will, he left one dollar each to his sons and the remainder of his estate to his wife and three daughters.[76] His wife had also been active in charities, including Carney Hospital and the House of Good Shepherd. Catherine (Leary) Prendergast died of pneumonia on 19 May 1901, also at 26 Brookford Street, Roxbury. She was buried at Mount Benedict Cemetery in West Roxbury.[77]

CHILDREN OF THOMAS PRENDERGAST AND CATHERINE COTTER

James	1847–[?]	
Jeffrey J.	1849–1925	m. Annie Ford
Maurice	1850–1851	
Maurice	1852–[?]	
James Maurice	1854–[?]	

---

72. Edwin M. Bacon, *Boston Illustrated* (Boston and New York: Houghton, Mifflin & Co./ Riverside Press, 1872). Available online at http://www.kellscraft.com/bostonillustrated/bostonillustrated08 .html.

73. Obituary, *Pilot*, 9 February 1895; Maureen Dineen, *The Catholic Total Abstinence Movement in the Archdiocese of Boston* (Boston: E. L. Grimes Co., 1908), 214.

74. Suffolk County Deeds, 2407:370.

75. Massachusetts Vital Records, 456:43.

76. Suffolk County Probate Records, Docket #98022.

77. Massachusetts Vital Records, 519:306; obituary, *Pilot*, 25 May 1901.

Daniel Leroy	1857–1920	m. Susan Malley
James Thomas	1859–1925	m. Margaret Mahoney
John	1859–1859	
Julia Elizabeth	1861–1925	
Maurice	1865–1865	
Mary Ellen	1866–1951	
Catherine J.	1868–1872	
Thomas Sebastian	1871–1951	m. Mary Hannon
Catherine Frances	1874–[?]	

Jeffrey J. Prendergast was born 6 September 1849 in Boston.[78] On 27 June 1872, he married Annie M. Ford, daughter of Daniel and Elizabeth Ford.[79] She was born on 17 June 1850, and she died before 1920. He began work as a harness maker, but by 1880 was working for the post office, where he eventually became a supervisor. As the first president of the Boston Post Office Clerks Association, he was active in agitating for better wages and benefits for the Boston postal workers.[80] He lived at 25 Dracut Street in 1900 and 9 Van Winkle Street in 1910. Jeffrey died on 4 April 1925 in Roslindale at the home of his daughter Mary Gertrude Hogarty.[81] He and Annie had eight children, six of whom were living in 1900.

Daniel Leroy Prendergast was born on 9 September 1857, the son of Thomas Prendergast and his second wife, Catherine M. Leary.[82] He attended the Bigelow Grammar School and graduated from Boston English High School in 1874, remaining involved in his class alumnae association for many years afterward. On 13 October 1880, he married Susan Malley, daughter of John and Susan Malley of South Boston.[83]

On graduation from high school, Daniel entered the employment of the Hamilton Manufacturing Company and Appleton Mills of Lowell, in their Boston office. He rose from the position of clerk to become the Clerk of the Corporation. In 1898, he left this position to work for the Boston Elevated

---

78. 1900 U.S. Federal Census, vol. 81, ED1526, sheet 4.
79. Massachusetts Vital Records, 246:110.
80. *Boston Globe*, 11 November 1888; *Boston Globe*, 9 September 1889; *Boston Globe*, 10 September 1894.
81. Obituary, *Boston Globe*, 6 April 1925; Massachusetts Vital Records, 1:275.
82. *Men of Massachusetts* (Boston: Boston Press Club, 1903), 325.
83. Massachusetts Vital Records, 318:146.

Railroad, where he was in charge of the real estate division. Over his lifetime, he held positions on the boards of numerous corporations, including the Brighton Cooperative Bank, Beacon Associates, the Somerville Horse Railway Company, and Eastern Cold Storage. His prominent employment status and social life resulted in his being listed in *Who's Who in New England* and *Men of Massachusetts*.[84]

Active politically, Daniel was involved with the Young Men's Democratic Club and was for years on the Democratic Town Committee of Brookline as well as the Democratic State Committee. . Among the charitable organizations with which he was involved were the Catholic Union, the Knights of Columbus, the Charitable Irish Society, the Clover Club, and other Irish social clubs. He was on the boards of four state tuberculosis sanitariums. He also belonged to the Boston City Club, the Exchange Club, and the Brookline Country Club. For recreation, he enjoyed horseback riding and motoring.

Daniel and his family lived in South Boston. Their most recent address there was on M Street until the family moved to 1726 Beacon Street in Brookline in 1905. At that time, he became involved in the founding of St. Aidan's Roman Catholic Church in Brookline.[85] His wife Susan died on 25 February 1913.[86] Daniel died on 28 July 1920 at their summer home at 5 Summer Lane, Atlantic Hill, Nantasket Beach.[87] Daniel and Susan had three children: Raymond Claude, born in 1884; Pauline (Prendergast) Doyle, born in 1895; and Harold, who died as an infant. Their descendants live in the New England region to this day.

James Thomas Prendergast was born on 16 June 1859 at 41 Albany Street. He was a twin of John Prendergast, who died as an infant.[88] He married Margaret A. Mahoney, daughter of William and Catherine Mahoney on 21 June 1893.[89] In 1880, his occupation was listed as bookbinder, but he later joined the Boston Fire Department. In 1900, he was listed as a hoseman at the Dudley Square station. In the 1910 census, he is recorded as working at Engine 46,

---

84. Marquis, *Who's Who in New England,* 873; *Men of Massachusetts,* 325.

85. Obituary, *Boston Globe,* 30 July 1920; William H. O'Neill, comp., *History of the Knights of Columbus* (Boston, 1897), 264-5.

86. Massachusetts Vital Records, 24:352.

87. Obituary, *Boston Globe,* 30 July 1920; Marquis, *Who's Who in New England,* 873; Massachusetts Vital Records, 55:160.

88. Massachusetts Vital Records, 125:119; Saint James Roman Catholic Church, Baptisms 1854–1864, p. 161.

89. Massachusetts Vital Records, 435:145.

Dorchester, and living at 46 Dix Street in Dorchester. He eventually rose to the position of lieutenant in the Fire Department. He died on 8 February 1925 at 25 Stoughton Street, Boston.[90] He and his wife did not have any children.

Julia Elizabeth Prendergast was born on 19 October 1861 and was baptized at St. James Church, Boston.[91] She attended Shurtleff School, Girls' High School, and Notre Dame Academy, Boston. She went to work as a clerk in 1889 for the Federal Court, and over her lifetime worked under U.S. Commissioners Henry L. Hallet, Francis S. Fisk, William A. Hayes, and Edward C. Jenney. In 1893, a committee of Chinese immigrants presented her with "a purse containing $40, a box of silk handkerchiefs, and a number of other articles from the residents of Chinatown." The gift was made in appreciation of her kindness and courtesy to the Chinese immigrants who had brought certificates to U.S. Commissioner Fisk.[92] In 1896, when she was the only court attaché present, she returned an indictment of Thomas Bram, who was charged with murder on the high seas. She was well known in the legal community and was considered an authority on practice and procedure in the federal courts. After an illness of one week, she died in her home at 98 Lancaster Terrace, Brookline, on 18 May 1925.[93] She never married and had no children.

Mary Ellen Prendergast was born in 1866. She went to work for the U.S. District Court in Boston, in Post Office Square, and was the deputy clerk for many years. She resided at 98 Lancaster Terrace, Brookline, with her sisters Julia and Catherine. She died in 1951. She never married and had no children.

Thomas Sebastian Prendergast was born on 20 January 1871, Washington Village, South Boston.[94] He married Mary F. (Mollie) Hannon in 1911. She was born in 1873. He was a purchasing agent at the Hamilton Mills, 77 Franklin Street, and by 1910 was the assistant treasurer. In 1940, he was an insurance broker at Employer's Liability Assurance Corp., Ltd., at 110 Milk Street, Boston. In the 1920 and 1930 censuses, he and his wife lived at 1240 Beacon Street, Brookline. He also lived at 98 Lancaster Street, Brookline.[95] He died in 1951 in Brookline. Thomas and Mollie had no children.

90. Massachusetts Vital Records, 1:109; obituary, *Boston Globe*, 10 February 1925.
91. Saint James Roman Catholic Church, Baptisms 1854–1864, p. 329; Massachusetts Vital Records, 143:123.
92. *Boston Globe*, 27 December 1893.
93. Obituary, *Boston Globe*, 19 May 1925; Massachusetts Vital Records, 9:134.
94. Saint Augustine Roman Catholic Church, Baptisms 1868–1883, p. 54.
95. Boston City Directories, 1910–1940.

Although many members of the Prendergast family were financially success-ful, politically active, and socially prominent, few produced heirs to inherit their legacy. Many descendants did not marry, and among those who did marry, few had children. The reasons for this unusual trend are unclear. Al-though James Maurice Prendergast circulated in the higher echelons of Bos-ton society, his strong Roman Catholic allegiance may have prevented him from marrying outside his religion. Perhaps the family's fortunes rose too quickly, outpacing their Irish American peers, and they found the pool of edu-cated, successful, and suitable mates greatly reduced. Nevertheless, a most valuable legacy has been passed on to all in James and Elizabeth's letters to their children. By providing a rare glimpse into their lives in Ireland and their children's experience as immigrants in the New World, the letters contribute substantially to the understanding of Irish Americans everywhere.

Glossary

Act of Union (1800): Following the 1798 rebellion in Ireland, the British government decided to abolish the Irish Parliament while maintaining Dublin Castle as the seat of government in Ireland. When George III refused to accompany the measure with Catholic emancipation, Prime Minister William Pitt and other cabinet members resigned in protest. After 1801, the main political issues were emancipation and repeal of the Union. The former was achieved in 1829, but Repeal was more difficult. It was only with the Anglo-Irish Treaty of 1922 that the issue ceased to apply to the present-day Republic.

Arbitration courts: In July 1843, Daniel O'Connell announced the formation of a legal system in Ireland which would be independent of the British government. Arbiters, including magistrates who had resigned or been dismissed by the government for supporting Repeal and others approved by the Loyal National Appeal Association, would decide cases brought voluntarily (and, therefore, constitutionally) before them by the Irish people, thus eroding British rule. No court fees would be charged. These courts operated for a brief time during 1843. (See letter #14)

Arms bill (1843): A "repressive bill giving the police virtually arbitrary powers of search and imposing the penalty of seven years transportation [banishment to a penal colony] for being in possession of an unlicensed firearm. The bill appears to have been something of a panic measure, presupposing preparations for an armed uprising or at least large-scale armed disturbances, although there is no evidence that any such preparations were afoot." *A New History of Ireland*, vol. 5, *Ireland under the Union*, *pt. 1, 1801–1870*, ed. W. E. Vaughan (Oxford: Clarendon Press, 1989), 184. (See letter #11)

Charitable Bequests Act (1844): This act allowed property to be bequeathed in trust for the benefit of Catholic churches and clergy. Trusts would then be administered by a board that included thirteen individuals, five of whom would be Catholics. The bill was strongly opposed by Daniel O'Connell and its passage was, for him, a political defeat. (See letter #20)

Corn Laws (1842): The Corn Laws were passed in 1815 as a response to the lobbying of Irish landowners who feared the collapse of grain prices at the end of the Napoleonic Wars. Tariffs were placed on tillage farming. In the spring of 1842, British Prime Minister Robert Peel introduced a new corn bill which reduced the amount of protection considerably. The Corn Laws were abolished by Peel in 1846. (See letter #6)

Currency: Twelve pence (12d) equal one shilling (1s); twenty shillings (20s) equal one pound (£1).

Famine fever: Typhus and relapsing fever (both referred to as "famine fever") were two of a number of opportunistic diseases which accounted for one million deaths in Ireland between 1845 and 1852. (See letters #29, 31, 32, 35, 36)

Famine relief: The potato blight that appeared in 1845 was so pervasive, and the Irish people so dependant on the potato, that it was clear the crisis would require government intervention. The British Parliament believed that providing relief to the Irish people was the obligation of the Irish landlords, and "poor rates" were collected to finance assistance. At first, assistance outside workhouses was prohibited and relief was available only through admittance to a workhouse. In 1846, public works projects were put into place, but they were generally ineffective. As famine conditions worsened, the Temporary Relief Act (1847) permitted relief outside the workhouses, and cooked food was then distributed. Relief committees administered programs locally. Several aspects of government relief policies are referred to in the letters. (See letters #26, 27, 28, 33, 34)

Godfrey family: The Godfrey family settled in Milltown in the seventeenth century, having been granted land there in the Cromwellian plantation. At the time the letters were written, the head of this important local family was Sir William Duncan Godfrey, the third baronet. The family home during this period, called Kilcolman Abbey (see letter #18), no longer exists. (See letters #13, 15, 16)

Know-Nothings: The informal name of the American Party, a political party of the 1850s whose nativist members held anti-Catholic and anti-immigrant views.

O'Connell, Daniel (1775–1847): Born near Cahersiveen, Co. Kerry, O'Connell turned his early success as a barrister to the campaign for Catholic emancipation, founding the Catholic Association in 1823 and eventually dominating nationalist politics. His stunning election to a Parliamentary seat for County Clare in 1828 led directly to the attainment of Catholic emancipation, earning him the title of "the Liberator," a term used by James Prendergast in the letters. O'Connell ranks among the greatest figures of modern Irish political history. (See letters #11, 13, 14, 17, 19)

O'Connor, Bartholomew (Batt), Fr. (1798–1890): father Batt O'Connor was born in Listowel, educated at Maynooth, and ordained in 1827. He was Milltown's parish priest from 1841 to 1886. His successor, Fr. James Carmody, in a brief history of the parish written in 1914, described Fr. Batt as "Of tall stature and commanding appearance . . . a fine specimen of the grand old *saggart aroon* [beloved priest]. Kindly, hospitable, witty, eloquent he was probably the best known Kerry priest of his day." The letters include references to Fr. Batt's trip to America (1847–1850), where he spent time with the Prendergasts in Boston. According to Fr. Carmody, Fr. Batt was in America at the request of Bishop Cornelius Egan, raising money toward the completion of the Killarney Cathedral. (See letters #11, 12, 14, 33, 36, 43, 44, 47)

O'Flaherty, Thomas, Fr. (ca.1799–1846): A Tralee native, O'Flaherty emigrated to America and became a physician, after having been educated for the priesthood at Maynooth, Ireland. He came from New York to Boston, where he continued his education and was ordained in 1829. He was a well-known figure in the Irish Catholic community of Boston during the time period of the correspondence. (See letter #2)

Peel, Robert, Sir (1785–1850): Peel was chief secretary for Ireland from 1812 to 1818, and served as prime minister from 1834 to 1835 and again from 1841 to 1846. He combined coercion of nationalists with conciliation of moderate Irish opinion and responded to the Great Famine with an effective relief program of public works and price controls. Unfortunately, the program was soon overwhelmed by the scale of the catastrophe, and with the repeal of the Corn Laws, Peel's party was split and he was driven from office in June 1846. (See letter #11)

Poor rates: In 1833, a commission was appointed to inquire into the poverty of the poorer classes in Ireland. The Irish Poor Law Act of 1838 set up a national administrative system for relief of the destitute poor. Ratepayers in each of the 163 Poor Law districts (unions) paid a tax (poor rate) that contributed to the support of paupers in a workhouse. Those who owned one-quarter acre of land or whose land was valued at four pounds or more were required to pay the rates. (See letters #4, 12, 13, 28, 39)

Potato blight: The first recorded appearance in Ireland of *phytophthora infestans,* an irresistible fungal disease, on the highly susceptible potato was in September 1845. (See letters #25–28, 31–32, 39, 46)

Potatoes: Though other crops were widely cultivated in Ireland, they were grown mainly for export. The potato was the crop on which laborers subsisted. Up to fourteen pounds of potatoes would be consumed daily by an adult male laborer. When it included milk, this diet was sufficiently nutritious. (See letters #4, 6–7, 10, 25–26, 28, 32)

> **Lumpers:** Though it produced a high yield, the lumper was of relatively inferior quality, but it was virtually the only variety grown by the poorer classes in Ireland for their own consumption in the years leading up to the failure of the potato crop in 1845. It was a thick, waxy, creamy potato, which was simply boiled, drained, and eaten communally from a basket, sack, or cloth. (See letter #6)
>
> **Minions:** A variety of potato also called "cup." "Minion" and "mingin" (see letter #6) are alternate spellings of "mingon." Letter #10 also refers to "black mingins." (see letters #6, 10)

Quill, John, Fr. (1790–1842): Milltown's parish priest from 1827 to 1841. (See letter #8)

Repeal movement: Founded in the 1830s by Daniel O'Connell, its aim the repeal of the Act of Union (1800), it evolved in the 1840s into the Loyal National Repeal Association. O'Connell proclaimed 1843 "Repeal Year" and through large public meetings sought to demonstrate overwhelming popular support. The British government banned a critical meeting at Clontarf, Dublin, in October and arrested O'Connell and his colleagues. O'Connell tried to revive the Repeal campaign after release from prison in 1844, but he was then in bad health and his efforts were overwhelmed by the economic and social catastrophe of the Great Famine. (See letters #10–12, 14, 17–22, 25–26, 31–32, 35–36, 40, 45)

Spring family: The Springs came into possession of the approximate area of the parish of Kilcolmen in the Elizabethan era. These lands were later granted to Col. William Godfrey in the Cromwellian plantation, and the Springs were then directed to transplant to Co. Clare, but the family remained in the area. The family of Francis Spring (1780–1868) is mentioned frequently throughout the letters. Francis, his wife Catherine, and their large family lived near Milltown in Castlemaine. Francis was the local land agent for the Godfrey family. His brother Arthur was in business in Boston during the time of the correspondence. There is a reference in letter #12 to the marriage on 5 October 1842 of Francis and Catherine's daughters Catherine and Anne to Arthur's sons Edward and Francis. (See letters #7–12, 17, 19, 21, 25, 26, 33, 45)

Workhouses: In the 1840s the workhouse system in Ireland was expanded. Workhouses were constructed throughout the country with provision for housing up to 100,000 people. In 1845, the first year of the Great Famine, 38,497 people were housed. In 1851, the same system housed 217,388. (See letters #38–39)

Young Ireland: A nationalistic movement, whose leaders included Charles Gavan Duffy, John Mitchel, Thomas Francis Meagher, and William Smith O'Brien, some of whom established the Irish Confederation in 1847. Through their writings in the Repeal propagandist journal the *Nation,* its members were highly critical of the government's response to the hunger in Ireland. In the summer of 1848, in reaction to government measures against them, they attempted to lead an armed popular uprising in Tipperary. The rebellion failed and Meagher and O'Brien were arrested, convicted of treason, and transported to Van Diemen's Land (Tasmania), as Mitchel had already been. Other members who participated in the rising escaped, including James Stephens, who would later found the Irish Republican Brotherhood. (See letter #39)

Further Reading

Bary, Valerie. *Historical Genealogical Architectural Notes of Some Houses of Kerry.* Whitegate, Ire.: Ballinakella Press, 1994.

Bourke, Austin. *"The Visitation of God"?: The Potato and the Great Irish Famine.* Dublin: Lilliput Press, 1993.

Connolly, S. J., ed. *The Oxford Companion to Irish History,* Second Edition. Oxford: Oxford University Press, 2002.

Cullen, James Bernard, ed. *The Story of the Irish in Boston.* Boston: James B. Cullen and Company, 1889.

Donnelly, James S., Jr. *The Great Irish Potato Famine.* Phoenix Mill, Eng.: Sutton, 2001.

Egan, Thomas, ed. *Milltown Parish: A Centenary Celebration.* Naas, Ire.: Leinster Leader, 1994.

Gray, Peter. *The Irish Famine.* New York: Harry Abrams, 1995.

Hickey, D. J., and J. E. Doherty, eds. *A New Dictionary of Irish History from 1800.* Dublin: Gill & Macmillan, 2003.

"Information Wanted: A database of advertisements of Irish immigrants published in the Boston *Pilot.*" http://infowanted.bc.edu/.

Kinealy, Christine. *The Great Irish Famine: Impact, Ideology, and Rebellion.* Basingstoke, Eng.: Palgrave, 2002.

McCarron, Edward. "Famine Lifelines: The Transatlantic Letters of James Prendergast." In *Ireland's Great Hunger: Silence, Memory, and Commemoration,* edited by David A. Valone and Christine Kinealy, 41–62. Lanham, Md.: University Press of America, 2002.

Miller, Kerby A. *Emigrants and Exiles: Ireland and the Irish Exodus to North America.* Oxford: Oxford University Press, 1985.

O'Connor, Thomas H. *Boston Catholics: A History of the Church and Its People.* Boston: Northeastern University Press, 1998.

O'Connor, Thomas H. *The Boston Irish: A Political History.* Boston: Northeastern University Press, 1995.

Póirtéir, Cathal, ed. *The Great Irish Famine.* Dublin: Mercier Press, 1995.

Ryan, Dennis P. *Beyond the Ballot Box: A Social History of the Boston Irish, 1845–1917.* Amherst: University of Massachusetts Press, 1989.

Vaughan, W. E., ed. *A New History of Ireland.* Vol. 5, *Ireland under the Union, pt. 1, 1801–1870.* Oxford: Clarendon Press, 1989.

Index